— Excerpts —

On the Meltdown: "We didn't know that at the highest levels of corporate America, there were business models that wouldn't pass muster in a lemonade stand. We kept hearing 'the fundamentals of the economy are sound.' The fundamentals are where we will sift through the rubble of the economy looking for our valuables."

On the Stock Market: "How can there be any confidence when there is no day of reckoning for failed business models? From the most powerful hedge fund trader to the simplest home owner, there is no reason to believe anything in the markets will work as advertised. There is no pool of speculators willing to risk their capital because lack of market discipline removes the foundation of every investor's decision to part with their cash."

On the Bailout: "We will endure years of economic hardship for a bank welfare program to pay for their negligence. And we have that gnawing feeling that the bailout is not really to recapitalize banks so they can feed us mortals more credit (which we're trying to quit anyway). The more likely reality is that the bail out money is really meant to reimburse wealthy investors for lost equity."

On the Recovery: "When government rewards the incompetence of fools by letting them live to trade another day, a viral infection comes imbedded in whatever limited recovery is forced to happen. The sacrifice required by letting the building burn to the ground and rebuilding from the ashes is just too difficult for the entitled generation."

On Fixing the Economy: "The road back depends on where we plan to return. The last two runs of prosperity, the dot.com boom and the housing boom, were both based on financial illusions. You would think by now we would have had enough of that. Apparently not. Long entrenched ways of thinking are not that easily undone. We're still looking for the easiest possible fix. After three decades of prosperity financed by deficits we are waking up to the reality of having no margin for error."

On Wall St: "The failure of US financial markets was bigger than the failure of deregulation or laxity of mortgage lending standards. At its core was a massive collective failure of morality."

On the Deficit: "We rode a wave of prosperity purchased on credit, and everyone owns a piece of that. Our politicians didn't talk about the deficit because we didn't."

On the Experts: "These so-called experts that rise up through the system into positions of power may be very smart and talented. At what, I don't know. Don't necessarily bet though, that they have a better grasp on reality than you or I. Anyone in a position of power who claimed the economy was sound in the three months leading up to the meltdown should be ashamed of their ineptitude."

On Income Inequality: "Between 2000 and 2006, 70% of income gains went to the top 1% of earners. A robust recovery will not happen until working class and middle class feel comfortable again."

On Stimulus Spending: "Yes, it will make the deficit much worse. Yes, we probably can't pay it back. But at least now we will finally be borrowing money for things of lasting value instead of just instant gratification. It's a start."

The Age of Entitlement

How Greed and Arrogance Got Us Here

*The Story of an Economy
Out of Control*

by Douglas P. Friesen

Copyright ©2009 by Douglas P. Friesen

All rights reserved

SBN 13: 978-0-9801725-9-1

ISBN 10: 0-9801725-9-4

Library of Congress Control Number: 2009925815

Manufactured in the United States

No part of this book may be reproduced, stored in or introduced into a retrieval system, or transmitted, in any form or by any means (electronic, mechanical, photocopying, recording or otherwise) without the prior written permission of the author or his agent.

Cover and Book Design: Lois Wood, www.loiswood.com

Editor: Eileen McAvoy Boylen

Published by

Speir Publishing
2200 Carlisle Ave.
Oklahoma City, OK 73120
www.speirpublishing.net

— Dedication —

To my mother, who had more compassion, courage, and conviction than anyone I will ever know; and who taught me from a very early age the importance of honesty and integrity.

Introduction 1

Chapter 1: The Entitlement Era 5
    Chronology of a Crash 5
    Entitlement Rules 12
    Self-Esteem Run Amok 14
    I'm OK, You're OK 15
    Lifestyles Out of Control 17

Chapter 2: The Creation of Money – A Background 21
    A Brief History of Money 21
    The Fed 25
    More Debt Equals More Money 30
    Bubble, Bubble, Toil and Trouble 33
    The Fed and Income Taxes 36

**Chapter 3: The Housing Bubble, or,
"Hell in a Handbasket"** 39
    The Perfect Storm 39
    Factor One: Low Interest Rates Fuel the Bubble 41
    Factor Two: The Deregulation of Debt 42
    Factor Three: A Worldwide Glut of Cash 46
    Factor Four: The Mortgage Sell-Out 47
    Factor Five: Debt-to-Capital Ratios Give Way 51
    Factor Six: Derivatives: The Next Big Meltdown 53
    Factor Seven: Greed Is Good,
    or "Let Them Eat Cake" 63

Chapter 4: The Aftermath **69**
    Blame It on Barney Frank? 69
    It's Never "Different This Time" 71
    The Bailout: Trying to Lose Weight
    by Loosening Your Belt 74
    Modified Limited Hangout 89
    "Too Big to Fail" Means Too Big to Exist 93

Chapter 5: Bubblenomics **97**
    800-Pound Gorillas:
    Social Security and Medicare 97
    Future Bubbles: Credit Card Debt
    and Commercial Retail Debt 105
    Those Who Fall Through the Cracks 107
    Entitlements and Complacency 112

Chapter 6: Hoodwinked and Hijacked **119**
    The Teetering Balance of Trade 119
    Robbing the Common Man 121
    Trickle-Down: The Failure of
    Supply-Side Economics 124
    All the President's Men 130

Chapter 7: Where Do We Go from Here? **137**
    The "Good Life" Is Hard Work 137
    Stop Doing Everything You've Been Doing 141
    There Are No Atheists in Foxholes 146
    Short Takes 148
    The Marketing Character 169
    The Final Word 171

— Introduction —

I'm a very unlikely author of any book, much less one about economic theory. I live in a quiet, small town, working in the construction trade, designing and building houses, and renovations to houses. My town is very old, incorporated in 1637. It was the second Pilgrim settlement in North America; they came here when the best farmland around Plymouth Bay was taken. The sense of history here gives you a different feeling as you're going about the business of living. The feeling that what you do matters, especially as a builder. All these years later, there is still only one traffic light in town. And, the streets are filled with very old houses, each with centuries of stories to tell. Not long ago, I stopped to look at a tiny little Cape near my house that I had never really noticed. Set on an acre of trees and gardens, the house has a pastoral setting so commonplace here you forget to take in the charm. Antique houses here have dateboards. This one was built in 1716. I paused to wonder how on earth this modest house could still exist?

The answer is generations of families who cared enough about that charm to pass it on to the next generation. The absence of those values is what bothers me most about what we are all about today. Nine out of every ten houses built here since the 70's are large, boxy colonials. They're not particularly charming and they all look pretty much the same. That is, except for those built since 1995, which look like they're on steroids. It's no longer about charm, it's about wholesale square footage.

It's through this lens I observed the crumbling of our economy. There were, in fact, clues that things were coming apart at the seams. But, the financial wizards told us the "fundamentals of the economy were sound." That litany of false confidence was repeated *ad nauseum* as pieces of the economy continued to fragment. It turns out the whole crazy thing had been operating beyond the bounds of sanity for quite some time, and we watched in subdued despair as our 401Ks were chopped in half for the second time in ten years. But, the most shocking thing of all was the surprise expressed by those in power.

Anyone paying attention could see the concentration of wealth and power at the highest levels, the enormous executive salaries and such. But, that's another world, far removed from our everyday lives. We knew the deficit was out of control and has been for quite some time. We knew Social Security was in trouble. And, there was this persistent noise about "subprime," like the last fly of summer that won't go away. Meanwhile, we saw a correction in home prices, and although this affected many of us, the correction was to be expected.

We **didn't** know that at the highest levels of corporate America, there were business models that wouldn't pass muster in a lemonade stand. Fundamentals? The fundamentals are where we will sift through the rubble of the economy looking for our valuables.

Introduction

If this was done with knowledge and forethought, "they" are guilty of greed and criminal fraud on a massive scale. It's almost worse if they did this unwittingly. It's no more comforting to think that the "experts," the titans of finance and industry to whom we've entrusted our economic well-being, are merely moronic.

As an unrepentant news junkie, I began to sift through that rubble. What I found astounded me. As it turns out, anyone with the common sense God granted animal crackers could have seen the truth that inexplicably eluded some of the world's smartest people. It was all there for anyone to see.

I never consciously set about to write a book. But there was a story here that I felt compelled to tell. At some point, right at about 10,000 words, I realized I was writing a book.

Here follows my disclaimer. I am not a financial expert. The facts and numbers in this book are the result of my sitting at the kitchen table for hundreds of hours, pouring over reams of internet information. I do not have a research staff. Mostly, I tried to verify the facts, figures, and concepts by cross-referencing, and by seeing them published in multiple places.

Because of the timely nature of the subject, the writing was done in relatively few months, by me sitting at that same kitchen table pounding on the laptop with my two index fingers. Most of the other fingers refused to cooperate, although I convinced my right thumb to operate the space bar now and again.

The Age of Entitlement: How Greed and Arrogance Got Us Here

Wherever possible, when I used more than a few words from something I read, I credited the author. My understanding is that "fair use" copyright laws grant that much. I am eternally grateful to all those web bloggers and editorialists out there who post information you tend not to see in print, or hear in prime-time media.

I am a simple man. I don't pretend to be an economist. My understanding of the complex financial world is average at best. In fact, I'm so simple I tend not to get in much trouble. Usually, I buy things only when I can afford to pay cash. When I borrow money, I make sure I can service that debt even in the harshest of times. Call me crazy.

If I misinterpreted some of the finer points, I beg forgiveness in advance. But, I don't think I'm wrong about the bigger picture I'm presenting. In fact, I challenge the smartest economic minds out there to tell me I am. Believe me, I would love to be wrong. It's no fun at all to be right about this stuff.

Doug Friesen
April 1, 2009

— Chapter One —

The Entitlement Era

> "It came with a speed and ferocity that left men dazed. The bottom simply fell out of the market... The streets were crammed with a mixed crowd — agonized little speculators,.. sold-out traders... inquisitive individuals and tourists seeking... a closer view of the national catastrophe... Where was it going to end?"
> — Account of the 1929 stock market crash in the New York Times

Chronology of a Crash

The economic crisis of 2008, although years in the making, started officially on Monday, March 10. It began very quietly, and it started with rumors. The word "on the street" (Wall Street) was that venerable investment bank, Bear Stearns, was having liquidity problems and was unable to cover losses in their mortgage securities. CEO Alan Schwartz, and Executive Committee Chairman Ace Greenberg, called the rumors "ridiculous." After all, they had almost $18 billion dollars to the good on their balance sheets.

By Wednesday, the rumors grew to a fever pitch. The stock, which had been trading at a low of $60, considered by some top stock analysts to be a "risky but good" buy at that price, dropped 50% to $30. A visibly shaken Alan Schwartz appeared on CNBC to calm the markets. His appearance had the opposite effect. It started a classic run on the bank, and by Friday, it was clear that without some type of intervention, Bear Stearns would be unable to open for business on Monday.

It was a sharp lesson in the value of confidence in the markets. Without it, rumors, unfounded or not, can destroy a company in days. It was also a sharp lesson for the Federal Reserve (Fed), who realized they would either become the lender of last resort, or allow the collapse of a Wall Street giant, creating major repercussions throughout the system, and causing untold damage.

During a series of tense weekend meetings, the decision was made for a backdoor bailout. Because it was an investment bank, not a regular commercial bank, (a bank whose primary business is providing financial services tocompanies), the Fed could not give money directly to Bear Stearns. Instead, the Fed gave $30 billion to JP Morgan Chase to "acquire" Bear Stearns in a shotgun marriage. By the weekend, Bear Stearns employees, who owned a big chunk of the company stock, were hoping to get at least $20 for their shares. The grim reality was revealed Sunday evening with the devastating announcement that Bear Stearns had been acquired by JP Morgan Chase for $2 a share.

When the Fed reviewed the Bear Stearns books, they found billions in hidden losses in "structured investments" like mortgage securities. More profoundly, they found Bear Stearns held over $20 trillion in "derivative" futures and options, a shockingly risky position that far outstripped their ability to cover even a tiny fraction of these contracts.

Chapter 1: The Entitlement Era

In May 2008, with the Bear Stearns rescue fading from the front pages, Federal Reserve Chairman Ben Bernanke called the subprime mortgage crisis "contained." Bernanke and many others anxious to return to "business as usual" clearly ignored warning signs throughout the summer of similar trouble at Fannie Mae and Freddie Mac, the two giant quasi-government mortgage companies. On September 7th, Treasury Secretary Henry Paulson finally announced the next rescue, the single most expensive government rescue in history. The Government agreed to spend $200 billion to restore confidence in Fannie Mae and Freddie Mac, whose stock had plunged 90% in a few months.

All of this government support for private institutions was beyond troubling to Paulson, a deeply conservative "free marketer." It represented what conservatives call a "moral hazard, " the worst possible breach of the very principle that defines free markets: the principle that self-preservation will cause even the boldest of players to step back from the brink of excessive risk. But, the markets were truly rattled. If huge companies like Fannie and Freddie could drop so easily, then no company was safe. The Fed had to choose between the "moral hazard," and an uncontrollable systemic failure among interconnected and interdependent worldwide super-banks. Nobody wanted that on their resume.

The Age of Entitlement: How Greed and Arrogance Got Us Here

The events of September 2008 unfolded like a slow motion train wreck. At first, the crash of some of Wall Street's biggest investment houses seemed cataclysmic enough, but the momentum of what came behind it caused devastation to the economy unimaginable just a few short weeks before.

Lehman Brothers was the next casualty, and they fell for all the same reasons: too many highly-leveraged positions in subprime lending and other high-risk investments. Potential buyers, including Korea Development Bank, Barclays, and Bank of America, had walked for one reason: the Fed would not guarantee losses on the deal. Paulson and Bernanke had "bailout fatigue," and they felt they had already gone too far with Bear Stearns, and with Fannie and Freddie. They had warned Lehman CEO Dick Fuld before, and now they aimed to restore some discipline to the markets. On Sunday September 14th, they made the "tough love" announcement that Lehman, an investment bank that predates the Civil War and survived the Great Depression, would be allowed to fail. Lehman's bankruptcy filing listed $613 billion in debt, making it 15 times larger than the largest bankruptcy filing ever, World Com in 2002.

On the same day, Wall Street giant Merrill Lynch agreed to be acquired by Bank of America. This, on the heels of Merrill Lynch losing an average of $52 million a day for an entire year, on now-toxic mortgage investments. Paulson issued a statement that the American people should remain confident in the "soundness and resilience of the American financial system." Some Wall Street columnists breathed a

Chapter 1: The Entitlement Era

sigh of relief Sunday night and submitted Monday morning columns saying the worst was over; the toxins had been purged from the system.

On Monday, September 15th, the world awoke to quite a different reality. We were not even breathing the same air. This is the day the world realized the systemic failure Paulson and Bernanke so feared had, in fact, occurred. Overnight, stocks in Asia and Europe had gone into freefall. Throughout the day, US stocks plummeted, with the biggest one-day point drop since 9/11. Credit markets froze solid on fears that no company or institution anywhere constituted a safe place to park money. My God, even some money market funds were in trouble!

By mid-week, AIG, one of the largest insurance companies in the world, was also suffering liquidity hell following its credit rating downgrade. Unwilling lenders would not save AIG from insolvency. Because AIG held default insurance (Credit Default Swaps) worth hundreds of billions of dollars on thousands of companies, their failure could trigger a cascade of further damage. The Fed quickly injected $85 billion to prevent a nuclear meltdown.

The week of September 21st, Wall Street's only two remaining investment banks, Goldman Sachs and Morgan Stanley, were forced to become "commercial banks" to make cash infusions from the Fed easier. It was the end of the era of Wall Street investment banks; they were all now regular commercial banks.

A bailout plan to restart the stalled economy was batted around Congress and presented to the public in a prime-time address by President Bush. It was met with resounding negativity by Bush's own party, and especially by the public. Very few were buying the notion that we had to throw money at rich people to avert an impending "apocalypse." The very same President Bush, standing at the very same podium, had invoked similar urgency to convince us we needed to invade Iraq five years earlier.

On Thursday September 25th, 119 years to the day after its founding, Washington Mutual, the nation's largest savings and loan, was seized by the FDIC for bankruptcy liquidation. The FDIC sold Washington Mutual's banking assets to JP Morgan Chase for pennies on the dollar, after Washington Mutual's stock price had tumbled 98% and depositors had withdrawn $16.7 billion in ten days.

Wachovia, once one of the most conservative banks in the US, was approaching insolvency and was in talks to be acquired by Citigroup. Wachovia ended up going with Wells Fargo, but Citigroup itself became the poster child for "banks too big to succeed," and later needed two massive bailouts. Meanwhile, Bank of America was reeling from shock after acquiring Merrill Lynch and having a close look at the books. Another cash infusion to Bank of America. Are we getting dizzy yet?

Through the weekend of September 27th-28th, Paulson and Bernanke met with congressional leaders to hammer out the "mother of all bailout plans." The message by Paulson

Chapter 1: The Entitlement Era

was clear: "If you do not act now, there will not be an economy on Monday." On Monday, the "economy" answered: Paulson, Bernanke and Congress are out of ammo and have lost control of the situation. The Dow dropped 777 points, the largest one-day point drop ever. Still, just to keep the present reality of a Dow languishing around 8,000 in perspective, the Dow was still well above 10,000 points.

October and November featured a worldwide banking collapse, and even the failure of an entire country, Iceland. Collapsing mortgage securities and the resulting credit crunch worked through the international banking system like a pig through a python. The depth of the sell-off was such that by year's end, the S&P index featured as many stocks that had fallen by at least 90% as ones that had risen at all. As miserable as all this seems, at a 50% drop (considerably more than any single year during the Great Depression), we were doing better than almost any other industrialized country, where most stock markets were down well over 50%.

Entitlement Rules

> *"Don't go around saying the world owes you a living. The world owes you nothing. It was here first."* - Mark Twain

Our free market system, even with its inherent greed and excess, was the model of dynamic wealth creation. Every stock market in the world wanted to be more like the US, and even Communist countries like China adopted the US model. In "bull" markets, the energy was infectious. In "bear" markets, corrections, and recessions, the momentum of free capital markets eventually cleaned out failing and underperforming companies, clearing the way for new growth. Even in the worst of times, the desire for wealth would always fuel human ingenuity to find a way to prosperity again.

Now, each new day dawns with new "all-time lows," new cutbacks, new drastic measures. The wholesale system collapse we are currently experiencing may or may not be worse than the Great Depression; that comparison has yet to play out. That we are even contemplating the comparison is testament to how far we've fallen. We are left to question the integrity of everything. In these stormy seas there is no holding ground to anchor in, no place from where we can start over. The collapse seems so deep, so bottomless, with potentially more shocks to come, one starts to envision some sort of Mad Max world. How did this all fly apart so easily; what really happened to cripple this giant?

Chapter 1: The Entitlement Era

We have spent most of the last two decades living through two booms: dot-com and now housing, both created easy wealth that disappeared even more easily. This can't be just a coincidence, there's got to be a trend here. Looking for the free lunch, we just can't accept a plodding path to prosperity. The bumper sticker for the age of entitlement is "I want instant gratification and I want it now!" And we don't seem to care how we get there, either. If we would have cared, this whole crazy thing would have set off alarms long before it did.

We might like to blame the whole thing on evil geniuses in ivory towers doing wicked things with their wicked money. There's probably more than a little truth to that, but it's a bit too easy. It lets us off the hook for any personal responsibility for what has happened. And, among the many admirable traits in short supply recently, personal responsibility is right up there.

Self-Esteem Run Amok

> "Too many people overvalue what they are not, and undervalue what they are." — Malcolm S. Forbes

The so-called "entitlement generation" is officially defined as "those born between 1979 and 1994, who believe they are owed certain rights and benefits without further justification." It's unclear how these dates came to define a generation, but it is clear that such a generation does exist. The rallying cry goes something like this: "We're entitled to have everything work for us, and if it doesn't, someone else is to blame."

We've all seen it: the biggest homes, coolest cars, best schools, the most stuff. Articles abound on how to deal with the "entitlement generation" in schools, colleges and workplaces. How did this happen?

Anthony Robinson, writer and speaker on spiritual matters, ponders this question in a May 2007 weekly on-line column, *Speaking of Faith*: "How has this pervasive sense of entitlement come to pass? Is it self-esteem run amok? Is it the emphasis on 'rights' in speech and thought? Is entitlement a corollary of affluence or a consequence of consumerism? Does it owe to being the world's sole superpower? Whatever the cause, this much seems true: Entitlement is the handmaiden of the ego, the sign of a neglected, malnourished soul. Entitlement signals a

Chapter 1: The Entitlement Era

rejection of the very DNA of America. Our national genetic code, at least at one time, was patterned on respect for the common man and woman. It was sequenced by a belief in the dignity of human life that's not the consequence of having, but of being. In the end, it's the entitled who, however rich, are truly poor. Instead of knowing life as a gift, life turns into something that's taken for granted — or worse, begrudged. That's real poverty, and no sense of entitlement can alleviate it."

I'm OK, You're OK

> "What others think of us would be of little moment did it not, when known, so deeply tinge what we think of ourselves."
> — Lucius Annaeus Seneca, 4 B.C.

If the 70s self-help book *I'm OK, You're OK* were written today, it might be called "I'm entitled, you're entitled." Somehow many of us, even those born before 1979, have come to believe we qualify for "the good life" whether we have earned it or not. Across the entire economic spectrum, there has been an excess of consumption and borrowing, with not enough production and saving. There was simply no way to use credit indefinitely, especially when most of the borrowing took place on the strength of home equity, which turned out to be mostly phony wealth. With traditional forms of saving at or below zero, consumers will now be forced to contract their lifestyles, and have already begun to do so. The July to September 2008 quarter saw the largest drop in consumer spending in 28 years. When 70% of the economy depends on consumer spending, it cannot absorb these imbalances without a profound recession.

Throughout history, America has witnessed the creation of the most dynamic economy in the modern world. Then something happened. Several decades ago, Americans stopped building wealth and started building debt. We stopped manufacturing things of value and became an economy that spins on the strength of consumption instead of production. Every generation has been taught to expect an improvement in lifestyle. Over the last 20 years, our personal consumption has risen at roughly the same rate as our personal savings have fallen, about half a percent per year. This is the first American era where consumers bought lifestyle improvement on the credit plan. Although economic models vary slightly, most show America currently has around a 0% savings rate, down from 12% in 1980. Meanwhile, the total household debt has skyrocketed from $4.4 trillion to somewhere between $9 and 10 trillion in just the last ten years. As a nation, we have a lot more "stuff" than any previous generation, and we are completely broke.

Chapter 1: The Entitlement Era

Lifestyles Out of Control

> "This would have been a big year for Darwin,
> if he had been fit enough to survive this long." — Grant Bartley

At certain points in history, like the period following World War II, debt, both public and private, has been wisely used to finance important economic growth. This current round of indebtedness seems to have served few purposes other than instant gratification. Easy credit, aggressive marketing and predatory lending... these are not the cause of our consumer credit crisis. These factors are merely symptomatic of a much larger problem. Several decades of stagnating or falling real wages have somehow coincided with an expectation of an increasingly material lifestyle.

The middle class family of the 1950s and 60s, even the 70s and 80s, grew up in a modest house of perhaps 1200-1500 square feet, sharing one bathroom and one car. It was normal for several kids to share a room. Since then, a 2400 sq. foot house with four bedrooms became the norm even while family size was decreasing. The "McMansion" syndrome spread across the country. In many areas, almost every new house built in the last decade was in the 4,000-6,000 square foot range, and houses much larger than that were commonplace. A car for each driver is a must, as well as a house filled with expensive gadgets and toys. This new lifestyle expectation took place not because we could afford it, but because that's what we expected to have. Those who profit from extending credit were happy to fill the void between "want" and "have." The end result of this credit binge was that by the end of 2008, one in every 171 houses in the US was in foreclosure.

In the midst of living fantasy lives we can't afford, we haven't been alarmed by government spending out of control. We haven't even paid attention. The same mindset that won't sacrifice current desires for future savings misses the contradiction between borrowing money from China to grow government spending while cutting taxes. The wake-up call will be the worst financial hangover experienced by any generation since WWII and the Great Depression. The fallout from consumers amassing huge debts for non-essential consumer goods, houses they can't afford, and government's inability to spend within its means will be unprecedented. And, it will inevitably fall upon on financially conservative taxpayers who were un-cool enough to live within their means. They will be the only ones with money left to bail out the hopelessly irresponsible.

In an interview on National Public Radio (NPR), Parker Palmer, a Quaker writer and theologian, speaks of "repossessing virtue" in light of the economic meltdown: "At some level, most of us knew [the economic crash] was coming. Who doesn't know that a society where the rich get richer, while the poor get poorer, is a society that will someday have to pay the piper? Who doesn't know that a society that encourages us to live beyond our means and refuses to regulate greed is one in which our avarice will come back to bite us? Who doesn't know that at every level of life, from personal to global to cosmic, what goes around comes around? The problem is not that we don't possess a capacity to know these things... The problem is that the knowledge we need, like the seismic shifts that create eruptions, originates underground. It comes from a place within us deeper than our intellects."

— Chapter Two —

The Creation of Money: A Background

> *"The modern banking system manufactures money out of nothing. The process is perhaps the most astounding piece of sleight-of-hand that was ever invented. Banking was conceived in inequity and born in sin... But if you want to continue to be slaves of the bankers and pay the cost of your own slavery, then let the bankers continue to create money and control credit."* — Josiah Charles Stamp (President of the Bank of England in the 1920s and the 2nd richest man in Great Britain)

A Brief History of Money

Most people assume they know what money is. Money is a placeholder for value and a medium of exchange. We think the government creates money, and most also assume it is backed up by gold or silver or some other monetary reserve. It's not. Relatively few people realize that the money now in circulation is not created by the government, it's created by a quasi-private bank called the Federal Reserve and it is not backed up by anything other than debt. Debt creates money, and it can be truthfully said that without debt, money would cease to exist.

At the risk of oversimplification, this is how money is created: When people deposit money in a bank, lending regulations allow the bank to loan a multiple of that amount of money to others, usually in a ratio of around

10:1. If you deposit $1,000 in the bank, the bank can then lend $10,000 to someone else. When that person uses the loan to buy a car and the car lot deposits the $10,000 in another bank, that bank can then lend $100,000 to another person. That original $1,000 very quickly becomes a very large sum of money that is not backed up by anything other than the borrower's willingness to repay the loan. Banks record these debts on their books as assets, although they are backed up by at least some capital (cash) according to ratios set by regulators. This used to be the amount of gold the bank had in reserve. Not any more. Money is no longer backed up or tied to the value of gold.

Modern banking regulations, called "fractional reserve requirements," determine how much money a bank can lend. These days banks are allowed to count not only the actual cash on hand, but also existing debt owed to the bank to calculate their reserves. It can then lend out ten times that amount. Part of the reason banks fail so easily is that their debt is now backed up by a very tiny cash reserve. And ironically, the more debt the bank "owns," the more assets it has and the more money it can create.

Our modern money system was created by The Bank of England in the 1600s to regulate the practice of "usury," or charging interest on money, which until then, many people viewed as outright thievery. This concept of leveraging of depositors' money by loaning it out stemmed from bankers' dissatisfaction with the amount of money they could make on the margin of deposit interest.

Chapter 2: The Creation of Money — A Background

The leveraging was based on the premise that all depositors never (or rarely) want their money back at the same time. Leveraging was a way for bankers to put "idle" money to "good use" and profitable purpose. Irving Fischer, economist and author, has this take on our money supply: "Thus the national circulating medium is now at the mercy of loan transactions at banks, which lend not money, but promises to supply money they do not possess."

The history of US banking begins with the founding fathers' wariness of a central bank. They lived through England's refusal to allow colonies control of their own money and the resulting War of Independence. The first Central Bank of the United States was modeled after the Bank of England and only marginally controlled the money supply. Still, the founding fathers were bitterly opposed. They called The Bank a vehicle for speculation, financial manipulation and corruption.

The Second Bank of the United States (SBUS) followed closely, with a similar make-up, except with more branches around the country. President Andrew Jackson spent most of his life fighting against the SBUS. Jackson hated and condemned bankers, claiming they only destroyed for personal profit and never built for shared prosperity: "You are a den of vipers! I intend to rout you out, and by the Eternal God I will rout you out. If the people only understood the rank injustice of our money and banking system, there would be a revolution before morning." Jackson succeeded in dismantling the SBUS, withdrawing the currency belonging to the government, and paid off the national debt for the first and only time in US history.

From 1835 there followed a period of "free banking," with banks competing from state to state. This era was characterized by instability and little uniformity of monetary supply. This instability led to yet another system of competing National banks that helped fund the Union effort in the Civil War.

Money panics, especially "The 1907 Panic," demonstrated the need for a central bank to better regulate money. Republicans wanted a central bank controlled by Wall Street Bankers, while Democrats wanted a reserve system owned and operated by the government. Then, as now, Republicans represented business and banking interests, while Democrats wanted government to sort out social and financial order.

Chapter 2: The Creation of Money — A Background

The Fed

> "I believe that banking institutions are more dangerous to our liberties than standing armies. If the American people ever allow private banks to control the issue of their currency, first by inflation, then by deflation, the banks and corporations that will grow up around the banks will deprive the people of all property until their children wake up homeless on the continent their fathers conquered." — Thomas Jefferson, 1802

In 1913, seven of the biggest bankers of the day met in secret on Jekyll Island, Georgia. At the time, these seven bankers controlled one sixth of the world's wealth. The meeting's purpose was to create a mechanism to control the wild market swings that had been occurring, such as "The 1907 Panic." The idea was to wrest monetary control from politicians with short-term agendas and put Republican bankers firmly in control.

The plan hatched at this meeting was the one Woodrow Wilson, a Democrat, reluctantly endorsed in return for badly needed campaign support. Democrats feared a central bank owned by New York bankers. What they got was a Federal Reserve Bank divided into 12 regional boards, allaying their concerns of Wall Street hegemony.

The Federal Reserve Act was passed by a hesitant Congress on December 23, 1913, when many lawmakers were home on Christmas leave. This legislation created the "Fed," a system of private banks owned and operated by private bankers appointed by the President, with the authority to act independently without prior approval from Congress or the President. It is a "fiat" system (money system based on value by government decree) of paper currency, although the value was originally tied to gold.

The name "Federal Reserve" makes it sound like a government institution, but it's really a group of 12 private banks that control the government's money supply. In fact, the name "Federal Reserve Bank" is a total misnomer. It is not federal, does not have a reserve, and is not a bank.

The officers of the Fed are nominated by the regional Fed banks and then appointed by the United States President to run the Fed for very long terms. This process was meant to ensure that The Fed would never be politicized. As a result, the Fed is accountable to no one, has no budget, is subject to no audit, and, no Congressional committee has knowledge of or can truly supervise its operation. Some have questioned whether the Fed is even legal, since there has never been a constitutional amendment stipulating the legality of the Fed to print money or control the money supply. The Constitution gives sole authority to Congress to "coin money and establish the value thereof."

The Great Depression was a test case of the Fed's ability to control financial panic. Depending on who's telling the tale, the Fed either caused The Depression, made it much worse, or both. After The Depression, the Fed's role continued to be loosely defined; its power and control waxed and waned over the years. It was 1951, when the Fed was given

Chapter 2: The Creation of Money — A Background

complete autonomy and independence from government oversight, a truly all-powerful Fed started to emerge. Our current financial structure came fully of age in 1971, when by executive order, Nixon uncoupled the US dollar from the gold standard, allowing the Federal Reserve to create unlimited amounts of money at will.

Some believe that the Fed is a sinister cabal of rich bankers bent on world domination, and others view the Fed as a benevolent force protecting us from inflation and the wild swings of an uncontrolled market. As with most things, the truth lies somewhere in between. But, there's no doubt that our money is controlled in secret, and we can never really know for sure which of those perspectives is accurate.

The Fed is no less controversial today than at the time of its founding. It is essentially a group of private bankers operating in secret, not answerable to Congress, manipulating America's money supply as they see fit. The government must pay interest on all of the money the Fed issues, which essentially means the government must pay interest on its own money. This interest, charged eventually to taxpayers, means that as the government's debt increases, the bankers who own the Fed get wealthier.

Since the Fed has never been audited, information regarding how much money is in circulation is hard to come by. There used to be a published report called M3 containing this information, but, in March 2006, the Fed ceased publishing it, claiming the collection process was too difficult and expensive. This move did not help the image of the Fed as a benevolent outfit protecting our money supply. The Fed could easily be an ATM for its controllers and we would never even know.

Congressman Ron Paul has long been a lone voice against the Fed and has sponsored numerous acts in Congress to abolish it. Paul suggests that the Fed has repeatedly and intentionally caused boom and bust cycles, caused by the inflationary pressure of creating money at will. It stands to reason that creating money dilutes its worth. It's as if you can generate value with a printing press. The name for that is "counterfeiting," and just like counterfeiting, the Fed's money machine doesn't create value, it destroys it. This steady erosion of purchasing power and value of savings represents a real, if hidden, tax on the working and middle class. How can a consumer-driven economy thrive when inflation-adjusted salaries remain flat for 30 years? The answer is: easy credit supplied by the Fed. In every boom and bust cycle, easy money supply fuels a bubble, enriching the wealthy and indebting all others, followed by a burst, whereupon the wealthy take their winnings and retrench until the next bubble. This is "bubblenomics."

Ron Paul, and others who advocate the abolition of the Fed, suggest that a return to the gold standard would prevent this boom and bust cycle. Without the ability to create money from thin air, credit would be tighter, and both people and governments would be forced to live within their means. Normal commerce could still take place, but the superheated frenzies tend not to happen with a money supply tied to something stable.

Chapter 2: The Creation of Money — A Background

As a brief Google search will tell you, some of the discussions about abolishing the Fed and returning to the gold standard suggest all manner of global conspiracies. But, there is no doubt that breaking from the gold standard in 1971 has unleashed an orgy of consumerism and debt, leaving everyone, including the government, close to bankruptcy. Everyone that is, except the bankers who own the debt. As Mayer Rothschild famously said in 1828, "Allow me to issue and control the money of a nation, and I care not who makes its laws."

There is nothing intrinsic about gold that makes it a magic cure for the money supply. Any other commodity or "basket of commodities" could be used. The idea is that a gold, or other standard, would make it more difficult for the government to artificially increase the money supply, which would prevent such mountains of debt from occurring. "Fiat money" is too easy to manipulate. It's just common sense that if the Fed owns the money and can manipulate money, they will manipulate money, and to the enrichment of those controlling the manipulation process. Why would it work any other way? A truly free country is one where the reward of hard work has an honest and predictable value that can't be so easily manipulated by the greed of the wealthy.

Tax cuts for the wealthy, the creation of enormous government debt, and inflationary boom and bust cycles are wealth redistribution on a vast scale. America is quickly returning to an oligarchy: an overwhelming majority of poor people, a small majority of wealthy people, and a rapidly shrinking middle class sandwiched between. People take the middle class for granted, but it didn't always exist as it does today. The great age of the middle class didn't happen through natural market forces, it was created by FDR's "New Deal" following the Great Depression. The continued existence of a robust middle class is not guaranteed.

More Debt Equals More Money

> "The Process by which banks create money is so simple that the mind is repelled." — John Kenneth Galbraith

In a monetary system based on debt, the worst thing that could happen is for everyone to repay all their loans. For individuals, paying off all debt would be desirable as it would free up money to spend on other things. But, if that were ever to happen in the economy at large, it would be a disaster, as with no debt, most money would cease to exist. Marriner S. Eccles, first Chairman and Governor of the Federal Reserve Board, said: "That is what our money system is. If there were no debts in our money system there wouldn't be any money."

The role of debt in wealth creation orders all other aspects of our financial system. Especially in the last few decades, America has voraciously consumed the debt offered by lenders. Personal savings in the post-World War II era have fallen from a high of 12% to negative numbers in 2008. American consumers have racked up $11 trillion of debt in a shockingly short time, and outstanding credit card balances alone average more than $8,000 per US household. America has prospered in the last few decades, but most of the wealth (created by debt) has gone to the very elite earners, the owners of debt. Much of the debt has been assumed by lower-income and lower-middle-income families, who borrowed aggressively to maintain their standard of living as real wages stagnated. Their debt has allowed the wealthy owners of debt to create even more money. The American consumer's appetite for material goods and debt has, more than anything else, led to today's widening wealth gap. Leo Tolstoy concluded long ago, "Money is the new form of slavery, distinguishable from the old only that there is no human relation between master and slave." The goal of "the few" who derive their wealth from debt is to convince "the many" to consume more.

There are economists who have advocated a monetary system based on something of real value. What a subversive idea! Republican, Ron Paul, advocates a monetary system based on gold or silver. That would limit government's power to inflate the money supply, and would force government to live within its means.

Right now the Federal Reserve can and does create money, as it is doing now with the recent bailouts. In Paul's thinking, this money has been created from nothing, is backed up by nothing, and has no value. The supply of money has been artificially altered by unreasonably low interest rates, which requires the creation of more money. That places no constraint on the supply of money.

The value of money is diluted when its supply is increased. Over the long term, this inflates the cost of everything we consume, which deflates the value of our wages. This loose credit makes it easy to buy ever more costly goods and sink ever further into debt. This institutionalized inflation results in huge windfalls for those on the right side of the curve, but that's usually not "us."

By their very nature, bubbles and busts drain money from low-income earners and the middle class for the benefit of the wealthy elite. For this reason, Paul regards the Federal Reserve as an institution whose sole purpose is enabling wealthy bankers to create money out of thin air, and to have taxpayers absorb the risk of doing so.

Chapter 2: The Creation of Money — A Background

Bubble, Bubble, Toil and Trouble

> *"For every man there exists a bait which he cannot resist swallowing."* —
> Friedrich Nietzsche

These built-in inflationary bubbles can never continue forever. Once people lose faith in the value of whatever is being inflated, be it houses, stocks or dot-com companies, the commodity very quickly returns to its real value in the marketplace. Bubbles pop after the wealth has been extracted from the system, and the public becomes collateral damage. We have come to accept this as the "business cycle," but Ron Paul and other detractors of the Fed believe that reinstating the gold standard would significantly diminish this built-in instability and still allow commerce to prosper.

Corporate America loves bubbles. They make money on the goods consumed and on the debt to consume them. Bubbles allow politicians (of both parties) to reduce taxes even though they are increasing spending. What a great way to get re-elected! When the bill comes due, blame the fallout from the "business cycle."

The theory is that deficits created by this runaway government spending, coupled with reduced revenues from tax cuts, will somehow be offset by the resulting prosperity. This is classic "supply-side" economics, a theory that production and supply are the key to economic prosperity, and consumption and demand are just secondary consequences. "Supply-siders" contend that low tax rates for the wealthy will stimulate growth and eventually pay for the resulting deficit. President Ronald Reagan embraced this as his economic mantra, and made it public policy. Governments of both parties have to a greater or lesser degree practiced supply-side ever since. For Republicans, it was part of their core ideology; for Democrats, they just never had an alternative coherent monetary policy. The ugly side of supply-side eventually emerges: the prosperity gets created in the form of a bubble because it is based on inflation, and bubbles always burst.

Supply-side worked well enough to lift the economic malaise of the 70s, and tax revenues did increase, but not nearly enough. The Reagan administration's deep tax cuts coupled with heavy defense spending created the largest deficit since World War II. The Reagan era deficits were only finally offset by the miracle of the dot-com boom. I do not believe we can entirely credit President Clinton with creating the 90s budget surplus, as many Democrats are fond of doing. Nothing that the Clinton administration did either created or sustained the dot-com boom, it was simply a function of the internet emerging in a climate ripe for bubbles. It was sheer good luck that the dot-com boom happened on Clinton's watch. But, at least he committed to a balanced budget by controlling spending and paying down the deficit, although he raised taxes to do it. Clinton left office with a $236 billion surplus, and surplus budgets projected (with faulty accounting) to last ten years into the future. He managed to do so just before the dot-com bubble burst.

Chapter 2: The Creation of Money — A Background

It did not take George W. Bush long to embrace the Republican tax cut mantra. But he also increased spending, which rapidly increased the deficit. In 2009, the deficit will top $1.75 trillion and is expected to remain at that level into the foreseeable future.

The next thing to drastically alter the economic picture was 9/11. In the stock market correction that followed, Bush stimulated the economy with some of the lowest interest rates ever seen. The timing couldn't have been better, as the American people had lost interest in the stock market and had a serious nesting instinct going on. Easy money and easy credit hid the ballooning deficit, as more wealth was created from thin air. Another miracle: people were rich with home equity and couldn't borrow and spend fast enough! US home ownership rates, which had risen only 2% between 1964 and 1994, shot up almost 5% by 2006.

Since the "Reagan Revolution" returned Republicans to dominance in the 80s, a curious feature of the party ideology has been its embrace of tax cuts without corresponding spending cuts. One might argue that Reagan felt compelled to win the Cold War through military spending. So, we might overlook that because he did shrink the non-military side of government. Even so, the deficit ballooned in an atmosphere of apathy. The topic came up, but without great alarm. Since then, an oddly asymmetrical conservative doctrine features tax cuts as an overriding imperative, but virtually abandons any emphasis on spending cuts. Conservative economic fundamentalism has been turned on its ear. "Big government" budget-busters like the 2003 $8 trillion dollar Prescription Drug Plan, traditionally a Democratic Party staple, were sponsored by Republicans and implemented under Republican control.

The housing boom which seemed so real? It was just another bubble. Big problem though... this bubble didn't erase the deficit like the dot-com one had begun to do. Because this bubble coincided with the Bush tax cuts, and possibly the largest increase in government spending by any Congress ever. The deficit doubled from $5 trillion to $10 trillion and counting in eight short years. My humble question ios: what is the next economic miracle we expect to pay down this deficit?

The Fed and Income Taxes

> "A system of capitalism presumes sound money, not fiat money manipulated by a central bank. Capitalism cherishes voluntary contracts and interest rates that are determined by savings, not credit creation by a central bank." — Ron Paul

In 1913 there was another monumental change to the American financial landscape. The 16th amendment to the Constitution legalized the collection of income tax. Until that time, the constitution had forbidden any direct taxation. Tariffs provided government funds, and because

Chapter 2: The Creation of Money — A Background

tariffs were tied to consumption, were seen to tax the poor disproportionally. Income tax is said to be a progressive tax, since the rates rise as income rises. In 1913, the first rates started at 1% on income of over $3,000, which meant that only the very rich paid income taxes. In fact, paying income taxes was seen as prestigious, an indicator of great wealth. At that time, income taxes accounted for only 10% of government revenue. What makes income tax a whole different ball game now is that rates start at 20% of income, and over 70% of government revenues come from personal income tax. The tax burden has been shifted from corporations to individuals.

It's no coincidence that we didn't need personal income tax until we needed to pay the Fed interest. The question remains, why would the government borrow money from the Fed and pay fees on it when it has the right to make money itself, interest-free? It's like taking money from yourself and then charging yourself a fee. The true extent of our indebtedness to the Fed is impossible to quantify, but those who advocate the abolition of the Fed estimate that 40% of our income taxes go to pay interest to the Fed. It follows then, that if the Fed were abolished and the government took charge of its own money, those interest payments could be used to pay off the deficit. After that, income taxes could be drastically reduced. Now that's an economic stimulus plan!

Before the creation of the Fed, America was a nation of independent "freeholders." Now, America is a nation of debtors, one step away from serfdom. This system of perpetual debt has been created to benefit those who profit from the debt. Remember that the colonists fought the Revolutionary War primarily because King George III would not allow them to control their own money. We are, in essence, cowards, compared to our forefathers who stood up and kicked the criminal bankers out of the country, and sacrificed their lives for American freedom. Currently, Ron Paul is one of the few speaking publicly about the Fed. Hopefully, our current economic troubles will cause a wider public discussion of the Fed's role in our lives.

— Chapter Three —

The Housing Bubble, or "Hell in a Handbasket"

> "The 'bubble' is a gross misnomer, a mischaracterization. The idea that we're going to see a collapse in the housing market seems to me improbable."
> — US Treasury Secretary John Snow, September 2005

The "Perfect Storm"

The housing bubble and the "subprime" mess are a good place to start sorting through the fundamentals of this so-called "sound" economy, since at first glance, this was the calamity that started it all.

The housing boom that started in the early 2000s was a bit of a surprise. The 90s dot-com bust and the resulting stock market crash and recession should have dampened our spirits. We learned there was no free lunch from an unlimited stock market boom. We should have humbly accepted that lasting wealth is not created so easily. But, we didn't. We were about to become fabulously flush with new-found real estate equity. Low-interest rates provided the fuel and the American dream provided the fire.

The delirium that followed had existing homeowners refinancing to lower rates, instantly creating wealth faster than even the 90s stock market run-up. What fun! New buyers got into the housing market and built equity that used to take decades in a few short years. Latecomers to the boom were afraid they'd miss out on the fun, and in a "sellers market," participated in bidding wars for any chunk of real estate worth owning. And, even many that were not.

Around this time, we started to hear the words "subprime," and, at first we weren't even sure what it meant. Did it have something to do with the prime rate? No, we learned it was people with bad credit getting mortgages from unscrupulous lenders. Well, stuff like that always happens in the midst of a market frenzy, right? It was a relatively isolated occurrence happening to people we didn't know in neighborhoods we didn't live in. No worries!

Except we kept hearing that word again. Always in the news. Subprime. Subprime. OK, we thought, this is going to be a problem and might even cause a recession, but it won't be long, and the damage will be limited to some banks that got a little crazy. Even after some rather large bank failures, Treasury Secretary Ben Bernanke, says so. Well, things like this always happen, it's the business cycle.

I can't remember when I realized the subprime was collapsing the economy and that everyone everywhere was in big trouble. It might have been after that multiple bank failure on Monday September 14th, but I think I still believed it was a big correction. It was some time after that when I realized the whole economy had been held together with bits of string and wire all along. It was something that crept into my brain slowly and almost imperceptibly, like a thief in the night. One day I woke up and thought "It's never going to be the same!"

Chapter 3: The Housing Bubble, or "Hell in a Handbasket"

My pet theory is that most calamities are caused by at least three things. One or two things are usually not enough for a calamity to reach critical mass. Just like the "perfect storm," seemingly inconsequential events collide and conjoin in unexpected ways to create calamities. As for the subprime mess, there are at least seven factors that can be readily identified.

Factor One: Low Interest Rates Fuel the Bubble

> *"Inflation is taxation without legislation."*
> — Milton Friedman

As discussed previously, the Feds lowered interest rates (12 times between 2000 and 2002) to stimulate the post-dot-com and post-9/11 slumps. Easing credit to unprecedented low interest rates injected huge amounts of capital into the system. Even though this type of capital injection historically creates unstoppable hyperinflation, and monetary devaluation, the high inflation numbers never materialized. Some of the inflation got sucked up by higher worker productivity. What happened to the rest of the expected inflation? The dot-com stock market plunge purged trillions of dollars of wealth, so there was no oversupply of money to create inflation. Let's print some more!

The Feds were watching for the first signs of inflation. They felt they could apply the brakes at any time to slow the thing down. But models don't always work as planned, and don't always provide the warning signs in time for the required correction. They did slowly raise interest rates, but not before a superheated housing bubble had created a lot of phantom wealth.

As for the dollar, it did experience a precipitous decline in relation to foreign currencies in this period. But things were going swimmingly, and everyone was enjoying the wealth a bit too much to worry about the value of the dollar.

Factor Two: The Deregulation of Debt

> "They who are of the opinion that Money will do everything, may very well be suspected to do everything for Money." — George Savile

The big push for banking deregulation started with Reagan's supply-side revolution. Government was the problem, not the solution. Notable debacles like the Savings and Loan scandal of the late 80s were early harbingers of the potential dangers of runaway capitalism, but this meltdown and others that followed seemed not to affect higher-ups in the banking sector. If anything, the cry for unfettered banking became more intense. Regulators and legislators were no match for the emergence of "super banks."

Chapter 3: The Housing Bubble, or "Hell in a Handbasket"

The policy changes that most affected the subprime boom took place in the waning months of the Clinton Administration. Hardly noticed at the time, these events caused much of the damage we are seeing today.

To set the stage for these events we must set the way-back machine to 1933. Congress passed the Glass-Steagall Act during the Great Depression, to sort out the mess created when ordinary (commercial) banks engaged in selling investments. Glass Steagall created a virtual wall between commercial and investment banking, and created the Federal Depositors Insurance Corp (FDIC). This wall remained in place for over six decades, until the 1999 enactment of the Financial Services Modernization Act, (also called the Gramm-Leach-Bliley Act). Republican Senator, Phil Gramm was largely responsible for slipping this into an omnibus spending bill, pushed by President Clinton and Congress to prevent a government shutdown during a budget standoff. Clinton has received a lot of the blame for this, although he was under pressure from a Republican Congress and still reeling from the Monica Lewinsky scandal. It wasn't that the Democrats made a conscious effort to deregulate; they were passively going along with the prevailing deregulation ideology in place since the Reagan era.

The act passed the House, mostly along party lines, with most Republicans in favor and most Democrats opposed. The bill that reached President Clinton's desk included a plum for the Democrats, a strengthening of the Community

Reinvestment Act. This was seen as an incentive for Clinton not to veto an otherwise unsavory piece of legislation. (The Community Reinvestment Act would figure prominently a little later in the subprime mess.)

The bill's main sponsor, Phil Gramm (later to become John McCain's Economic Advisor) was the prime mover behind the Financial Services Modernization Act. In fact, Gramm has been called "the high priest of deregulation," and the Washington Post recently named him as the number two person responsible for the economic crisis of 2008 (behind Alan Greenspan).

Deregulation ran in the Gramm family. Phil's wife Wendy had just come off five years as head of the Commodity Futures Trading Commission, where she used her husband's connections to push through a companion piece of deregulation, the Commodity Futures Modernization Act. This is the act most responsible for deregulating derivatives trading like "Credit Default Swaps," and was passed on December 15, 2000, the last day before Christmas recess, without any discussion, and with only a voice vote.

Bush had already won the election, and Clinton, serving out his last days, was in no position to veto. It's worth noting that this bill also contained a piece called the "Enron Loophole" that exempted companies like Enron from oversight in trading energy derivatives. After her stint on the CFTC, Wendy Gramm went on to sit on the Enron Board and made $1.8 million trading these derivatives. Democrats tried repeatedly and unsuccessfully

Chapter 3: The Housing Bubble, or "Hell in a Handbasket"

to close the "Enron Loophole" before the loophole eventually consumed Enron in a spectacular collapse.

It's unlikely that many lawmakers ever read these bills, or understood their relevance. Even if they did, the dynamics of the time tilted toward unhindered free markets. A sense of entitlement left almost everyone involved uninterested in the implications of such a monumental change to investment regulations. In recent interviews, President Clinton still denies that these deregulatory measures had anything to do with the subprime crisis.

Suddenly commercial banks could sell their debt as investment products, and Wall Street began selling debt-backed securities. Just as a paper bank note (a dollar bill) represents a promise to pay; mortgage paper, also a promise to pay, became a "currency" that was securitized into investments and circulated worldwide, just like a paper dollar. These investments were highly regarded, as they were backed up by something tangible (real houses), which is more than you can say for US government money.

Factor Three: A Worldwide Glut of Cash

> "I am opposed to millionaires, but it would be dangerous to offer me the position." — Mark Twain

These securities became popular during a time when the pool of investment capital grew exponentially. The growth resulted from many factors, including countries around the globe flush with cash from free trade, and the surging economies of underdeveloped nations. The worldwide pool of available investment capital, that is, the savings of the entire world, took all of recorded history to become $36 trillion dollars as of 2000. Six years later, it had doubled to $72 trillion. Investors, especially institutional investors, grew to love these mortgage securities. In a low interest rate environment, they offered returns higher than US treasury bonds (the "gold standard" of investing) and seemed very safe.

Moody's and other rating services designated these securitized debt investments "triple A." Problem was, the ratings were not independent; the underwriters were working with the rating services to package these loans in a palatable form. Because these mortgage securities were popular among investors, they were obviously embraced by bankers and brokers because they offered high payouts and were easy to sell. This created a demand for more mortgages, which coincided nicely with the lowest mortgage rates ever. That, and the "nesting" instinct. People couldn't

Chapter 3: The Housing Bubble, or "Hell in a Handbasket"

spend enough on homes and home improvement. Even with a record number of Americans refinancing and getting new mortgages, demand by investment groups for new securitized mortgages was outstripping supply. It was at this point that greed turned the American Dream into a nightmare.

Factor Four: The Mortgage Sell-out

> "Opportunity may knock only once, but temptation leans on the doorbell."
> — Author Unknown

The details and timing of what followed will be dissected in more detail by historians, but it went something like this: The frenzied climate surrounding the mortgage industry created what amounted to mortgage "sweatshops." Brokers were pressured for more mortgages than could apparently be delivered. Lending standards were gradually but relentlessly lowered, and the grisly details filled nightly newscasts in 2006 and 2007.

Some of these scenarios included hotel suites in Las Vegas filled with 40 loan approval officers paid on a piecework basis with a mandate to approve one loan per hour. For every bundle of loans there were huge bonuses for everyone. The brokers pulled down several hundred thousand, even million dollar salaries. The scenario included appraisers giving brokers whatever appraisal numbers they requested to make the loan fit the investment package, lest the appraiser be cut from the gravy train.

There were mortgages with no money down, no proof of income, low "teaser" rates, and adjustable rates, given to people (not always poor) who had less than exemplary ability to pay the mortgage over time. Especially if the interest rates increased or the value of the house declined. "No money down" loans were accomplished with a sleight of hand called "piggyback," a second mortgage taken out with the first to pay the down payment. In 2000, Standard and Poor's actually endorsed this type of loan as "no more likely to default than a regular loan," and allowed 20% of the bundled mortgages to contain such loans. It is hard to imagine anyone arriving at this conclusion. Even in a rising market, the time required to build enough equity to cover the down payment, let alone pay down the principle, would be many years.

Before this time, the subprime market had been about 3-5% of the mortgage market, and fulfilled a useful role. It gave people who wouldn't qualify for a variety of reasons (like self-employment), but could carry a mortgage, the opportunity for home ownership. In return, they paid a higher rate to offset the greater risk. By itself, it was a sound and useful business model. But by the time the subprime market was fully wound up, it was 15% of the mortgage market, and the criteria for getting a mortgage was little more than having a pulse.

Chapter 3: The Housing Bubble, or "Hell in a Handbasket"

The subprime tsunami happened not at just one or two firms, but dozens, even hundreds. Brokers who resisted the tide were quickly consumed by it. When nightly newscasts and financial advisors warned the public about these dangerous subprime loans, most people probably viewed this as an isolated practice by a few unscrupulous people. Few had any idea of the magnitude of what was happening. Few that is, outside the tight circle of mortgage originators, appraisers, mortgage bundlers, and investment houses, all of whom were making an awful lot of money. Twenty-one-year-old mortgage brokers were buying summer houses in the Hamptons. Sales meetings featured $1,000 bottles of champagne.

These mortgages were being sliced and diced into securities, making the loans essentially untraceable. The mortgage originators, bundlers and bankers had nothing but ethics to keep them from collecting as many mortgage commissions as possible, at any cost. Investment houses, now loosely regulated institutions, could then chop the mortgages into pieces and sell them to unsuspecting investors.

The role of the rating services cannot be understated. The loans were being bundled and rated according to their associated risk, but the rising market was seen to mitigate the risk of the worst bundles, or so called "tranches," if they were mixed with "less risky tranches" and given Triple A ratings. A Congressional panel recently uncovered internal email exchanges at Standard and Poor's like this one: "Let's hope we are all wealthy and retired by the time this house of cards falters." One employee complained to his superiors that the easy approvals made company analysts appear incompetent or like we had "sold our souls to the devil for revenue." If this ratings subterfuge had not occurred, thousands of pensions and mutual funds would never have purchased mortgage-backed securities, and hedge funds would have been more cautious. Even mortgage lenders would have retreated with no one to buy their mortgages and peddle them to investors. The market had become so complex that even sophisticated money managers had to rely on the rating services to analyze these securities. It's not that the rating services just botched a few calls. They systematically disguised risk when their job was to expose it.

Any rational person would wonder how on earth this could continue for so long without tripping the alarm. In the case of high-profile fraud like Enron's, it is entirely possible only a handful of people knew what was really going on. Here, hundreds and hundreds of people at every level were feeding the monster. Perhaps the naive bought into the idea that if housing prices continued to rise forever, it would all work out for everyone, including the borrowers. Perhaps most just didn't really understand. These "Structured Investment Vehicles" were now so complicated that a single deal might run to 300 pages. Good and bad investments were mixed and ground into sausage. The most predatory among the lot surely knew how the numbers might crunch, because they are in the business of crunching hypothetical numbers. Greed, unchecked, had worked its magic at every level of the system.

Chapter 3: The Housing Bubble, or "Hell in a Handb

By 2005 and 2006, more media reports were surfacing, such as Gretchen Morgenson writing in the *New York Times* of Merrill Lynch staffers being penalized if they warned of risk. Internal credit controls were consistently and deliberately weakened. Way back in 2002, all 50 state Attorneys General warned the Bush administration of predatory lending practices that they feared would lead to a collapse. Far from being concerned, the Bush administration in 2003 invoked a clause they dug up from the 1863 National Banking Act, essentially nullifying state predatory lending laws. And, they even created new rules preventing states from enforcing existing consumer protection laws against national banks.

Factor Five: Debt to Capital Ratios Give Way

> "When I have money, I get rid of it quickly,
> lest it find a way into my heart." — John Wesley

The "trifecta" of deregulation was achieved in 2004 when the SEC, weakened by poor investigators, an ineffective executive, and relentless lobbying by powerful banking interests, waived its "net capital rule." Previously, investment banks were prevented from recklessness by being required to cover 10% of their risk with actual money. Former Treasury Secretary, Henry Paulson, was one of the biggest lobbyists against this requirement when he was CEO of Goldman Sachs. Now there would be no limit to risk these banks could take on. The idea was that these sophisticated financial instruments were traded only by rich investors too savvy to need protection. In place of the "net capital rule," which banks considered "onerous," a voluntary risk management system was set up, but never effectively enforced. This system was totally dismantled in September 2008 by current SEC Chairman, Christopher Cox, days before the big meltdown.

The big investment houses immediately jacked up their ratios to as much as 40:1. Unverified media reports had Fannie and Freddie leveraged as much as 100:1. When Lehman Brothers failed in September 2008, they were leveraged at 33:1. To give some idea of how risky that position is, consider this: at 33:1, a 3% drop in the value of the (debt) asset will wipe out the capital and make the firm insolvent. Lehman, whose lineage goes back into the 1800s, was essentially betting its entire past and future against a small downtick in the market. Even historically super-conservative firms like Wachovia and Washington Mutual were in on the game in a big way.

Chapter 3: The Housing Bubble, or "Hell in a Handbasket"

Factor Six: Derivatives, The Next Big Meltdown

> *"If you make money your god, it will plague you like the devil."*
> — Henry Fielding

As Bob Seger sang in his 1980 classic, "Against the Wind": "I wish I didn't know now what I didn't know then." Right back at you, Bob. If not for greed on a level few can comprehend, we would never have heard of "Collateral Debt Obligations," "Credit Default Swaps" or any of the arcane terms describing investment vehicles so complex almost no one claims to properly understand them.

If the subprime mess had been just a tsunami it could probably have been contained as just that, a "mess," like the Savings and Loan Scandal. But it was more than that. The sixth factor made it into an earth-shattering event. The sixth factor was the boom in the use of derivatives, exotic financial instruments that derive their value from something else. These instruments call for money to change hands at some future date: the amount to be determined by one or more reference items, such as interest rates, stock prices, or currency values. Many derivatives are speculative bets against a small change in the value of something over a short term, but some are bets against far-reaching unknowable circumstances and the resulting consequences.

These derivatives became highly profitable, and hedge funds benefited enormously from this stuff. One hedge fund manager, John Paulson (no relation to the Treasury secretary), "earned" $3.74 billion in 2007, which works out to approximately $1.7 million per hour! Alan G. Hevesi, the New York State comptroller, announced in 2005 that Wall Street bonuses were estimated to hit a record $21.5 billion, surpassing the previous record of $19.5 billion set in 2000. Those bonuses resulted from record profits at many of Wall Street's major investment banks, including Goldman Sachs, Bear Stearns and Lehman Brothers, the very banks who would either fail or require bailout less than three years later. Even now, despite government and public pressure, and with the economy imploding, the 2008 bonuses at Morgan Stanley and Goldman Sachs alone are reported to be in the $13 billion range. In fact, in a bizarre twist, the 2008 salaries and bonuses at Morgan Stanley exceeded their market capitalization. In other words, Morgan Stanley's value in the stock market was less than salaries and bonuses paid out that year.

In the world of derivatives, perhaps none are more risky than the Credit Default Swap. "CDS's" are a type of derivative, an elaborate insurance policy which hedge against a debt default. These instruments are themselves traded like securities, by companies betting against the risk. The entire value of this market is only hinted at, since it is almost completely unregulated. The "guesstimated" potential value (if they all had to be fulfilled) run from $45-60 trillion, which is many times larger than the stock market itself. In fact, it dwarfs the stock and bond markets.

Chapter 3: The Housing Bubble, or "Hell in a Handbasket"

Think of it like this: You own a house and buy insurance in case it burns down. For the insurance company, one house burning down doesn't necessarily increase the risk of any other fires. But, suppose many of your neighbors have made expensive bets that your house might burn down. These bets, "the hedge," become risks themselves. Instead of insuring against risk, the swaps became a way of speculating on corporate credit. These swaps have been traded so vigorously, and are so complex, that it is often unclear who owns them and whether they can in fact be honored in the event of a default. If anyone had taken the time to add up what was insured and who could cover it, the numbers would have been so absurd that no one would have bought the damn things.

AIG went heavily into this new twist in insurance products. After all, who knows insurance better than they do? Besides, it was hugely profitable. Problem was, the whole thing was an impossibly complex chain of ownership and obligation, and when the music stopped, holders of these swaps, like AIG, found themselves out there with $445 billion worth of bad swaps, $58 billion relating directly to the subprime market. When auditors examined the books in early 2008, they declared the management "not in control of their 'derivatives.' " For their part, management declared they could not "reliably quantify losses."

The credit default swaps that AIG sold were insurance against a specified risk, but with a few interesting twists. The companies (called counterparties in insurance parlance) taking out the insurance were large banks or institutional investors placing large amounts of money into play in the markets. In the case of a bank, these investments show up as an asset on the balance sheet. In order that the bank remains solvent irrespective of the performance of its "assets," they are required to keep a specified amount of capital (cash) on hand as collateral to cover potential losses. By taking out Credit Default insurance against that potential loss, the banks were able to circumvent those capital requirements, freeing up the cash to buy more investments.

The devil is always in the details, and it was the fine print that caused these swaps to turn so ugly, so fast. The insurance that covered these now popular mortgage and debt securities was written not only to pay out if the debt securities defaulted, but even if they went down in value. It is as if you could buy gambling insurance that you would never lose at the crap tables.

The problems at AIG's end of the transaction were even more complicated than just paying out enormous sums of money they didn't have. AIG was the largest insurance company in the world, with a triple A rating, the highest rating possible. In fact their rating was so good, they also were not required to post collateral, in their case, to cover possible payouts of these policies. When the investment securities started to

Chapter 3: The Housing Bubble, or "Hell in a Handbasket"

sour, and they were suddenly forced to pay out billions to cover these swaps, their rating was reduced to double A. Still pretty good. But, the fine print required them to post collateral if their credit rating was reduced. This, at a time when they didn't even have enough money to pay the claims, let alone post collateral.

The whole mess unraveled very quickly and destroyed one of the world's great companies. It was largely the action of one small branch of this enormous company, the London-based Financial Products Division, Why would AIG sell such a product? It appears they never "war-gamed" their business model for any contingency situations at all. These Credit Default swaps could only work if the housing market and their associated mortgage securities were an asset class that would continuously rise in value. Even a slight downtick could be a disaster. All the economic activity surrounding the housing bubble seemed to have operated in this same strange vacuum.

The enormous size of AIG and the potential effect of this "loss of confidence," if not AIG's outright default, was a major factor in triggering the global financial crisis. Some suggested that because AIG had underwritten so much risk on so many companies, their failure could cause global markets to cease functioning altogether. Bloomberg News reported that shortly after leaving Wall Street as Goldman Sachs CEO in 2006, Henry Paulson was at Camp David warning the president and his staff of "over-the-counter derivatives as an example of financial innovation that could,

-57-

under certain circumstances, blow up in Wall Street's face and affect the whole economy." Today, some feel that derivatives could be the next big meltdown that should it occur, would be devastating on a massive scale. A conservative estimate of the value of the entire market is at least $300 trillion, but could be as much as $770 trillion. No one really knows, as the information comes from a voluntary canvas of the players in that market, and there are no reporting requirements of any kind to any regulatory body.

The potential volatility of this market can be seen by example. One of the first spectacular implosions was Orange County, California, which lost $1.6 billion in 1994 because of derivatives traded by just one man, bankrupting the county. Following that was Long Term Capital Management, which disintegrated in 1998 with a stunning $1.4 trillion of derivatives on its books, backed up by only $4 billion of asset value. The potential miscalculations can have staggering consequences, as with the hedge fund Amaranth Advisors losing $4.6 billion (half its value) in two days by miscalculating the price of natural gas futures.

When some of these earlier companies went under, only a handful of banks had that kind of exposure. Now, hundreds do. Billionaire investor George Soros has said of derivatives, "we really don't understand how they work." Investor Warren Buffett, the second richest man in the world, called them "financial weapons of mass destruction." The derivatives market in its current form, with its pervasive entanglement across the investment spectrum,

Chapter 3: The Housing Bubble, or "Hell in a Handbasket"

has never been tested against big market swings, (before now) and represents a huge, almost incalculable threat to long-term global financial security.

Following the collapse, it was a sad and pathetic sight to watch Alan Greenspan testify to Congress that the derivative contracts themselves were "sound," but that greed had overrun the system. Brilliant, Sherlock. Greenspan had convinced himself that although it was apparently quite easy to make untold billions exploiting loosely-regulated markets, somehow personal integrity and honor, or failing that, self-preservation, would prevail. How shallow to blame the market's participants rather than the regulatory regime he himself ruled.

Derivatives, which caused more failure than any other single element of the crisis, had no stauncher defender than Greenspan. Speaking before the Senate Banking Committee in 2003, he claimed it would be a mistake to more closely regulate them: "What we have found over the years in the marketplace is that derivatives have been an extraordinarily useful vehicle to transfer risk from those who shouldn't be taking it to those who are willing to and are capable of doing so." While financial titans like George Soros and Warren Buffett were warning against the dangers of derivatives, Greenspan was touting their value in calming the markets: "Not only have individual financial institutions become less vulnerable to shocks from underlying risk factors, but also the financial system as a whole has become more resilient."

Columnist and best-selling author, Michael Lewis, quotes such notables as former Fed member and Princeton economist, Alan Blinder, characterizing Greenspan as "a consistent cheerleader on derivatives." Lewis also quotes former SEC Chairman, Arthur Levitt Jr., as saying "Mr. Greenspan opposes regulating derivatives because of a fundamental disdain for government." According to Lewis, Levitt also said that Mr. Greenspan's authority and grasp of global finance consistently persuaded less financially sophisticated lawmakers to follow his lead. "I always felt that the titans of our legislature didn't want to reveal their own inability to understand some of the concepts that Mr. Greenspan was setting forth," Mr. Levitt said. "I don't recall anyone ever saying, 'What do you mean by that, Alan?' "

Lewis goes on to to describe Representative Ed Markey (D-MA), one of the few who got it, requesting an investigation into the risk of derivatives by the General Accounting Office (GAO). The resulting report was damning in the extreme. It stated, "liquidity problems in the markets... could result in a financial bailout paid for or guaranteed by taxpayers." Markey sponsored a regulatory bill that was never passed. The stock market surged as congressional lawmakers with non-existent expertise credited the good times to Greenspan's steady hand. Texas Republican, Phil Gramm, whose "steady hand" was involved in almost everything that's gone wrong with the stock market, gushed to Greenspan "You will go down as the greatest chairman in the history of the Federal Reserve Bank."

Chapter 3: The Housing Bubble, or "Hell in a Handbasket"

In 1997, the Commodity Futures Trading Commission (CFTC), headed by Brooksley Born, began a big push to regulate derivatives, calling for greater disclosure of trades and more reserves to cushion against losses. She was part of a "working group" along with Greenspan at the Fed, Robert Rubin at Treasury, and SEC head, Arthur Levitt, looking into regulation of derivative trading.

Born had strong disagreements with her colleagues right from the start, but as a practiced trial lawyer, (at one time on the short list for Clinton's Attorney General), she was not about to back down. Born testified before Congress at least 17 times, relentlessly warning of the risk of ignoring derivatives. But she was not considered a Wall Street insider and certainly not part of the "Boy's Club." Her proposal was fiercely attacked by Greenspan, Rubin and Levitt, who told her she didn't know what she was doing. Rubin's successor at Treasury, Larry Summers (presently chairman of Obama's Economic Council), petitioned Congress to make sure Born's proposals never saw the light of day. Summers warned of "casting a shadow of regulatory uncertainty over an otherwise thriving market."

In 1998, Ms. Born's apprehensions became reality, as Long Term Capital Management (LTCM) imploded as a result of derivatives trading. Two days later, Born warned the House Banking committee: "This episode should serve as a wake-up call about the unknown risks that the over-the-counter derivatives market may pose to the US economy and to financial stability around the world." She spoke of an "immediate and pressing need to address whether there are unacceptable regulatory gaps."

The 1998 LTCM meltdown didn't change anything. Traders were making huge amounts of money on derivatives and politicians were loath to upset something very lucrative that, by the way, they didn't really understand. Politically isolated and burned out, Born left the CFTC shortly thereafter. With the lone dissenter gone, the others in the working group pushed a proposal through Congress, stripping the CFTC of any regulatory authority over derivatives. The proposal went through on stealth mode, attached to an 11,000-page appropriations bill, the same one that eliminated the Glass-Steagall Act. Various proposals on self-regulation for the derivatives market were bandied about by the working group, but ultimately, nothing substantial was done.

Rubin now claims he was concerned about derivatives way back in his Goldman Sachs days, but didn't air his concerns because no political will for action ever existed. Summers and the others who refused to regulate derivatives have also now expressed regret, but they blame the Fed, saying Greenspan was adamantly opposed to any regulation. Even President Clinton says now that he regrets he did not do more to help Born but "we didn't have the political capital." There was also an undeniable "glass ceiling" aspect to this. The inability of the male power brokers to regard a woman as an equal partner played a large role. If Robert Rubin, or any of the other

Chapter 3: The Housing Bubble, or "Hell in a Handbasket"

(spineless) males, had shown the courage of their belatedly-expressed convictions, history might have played out very differently.

These derivatives were so revered by Wall Street, they were viewed as nothing short of the "second coming" and the cure for all ills. The huge corporate mergers happening at the time, and the resultant concentration of wealth, were not a threat according to Greenspan, because "the risks had been hedged by derivatives." Talk of a housing bubble was dismissed because derivatives "caused a sharing of risk with other firms." Ironically, it was this same "sharing of risk" that eventually made the crisis go viral and infect the entire world. Greenspan was still unapologetic in a postscript to his memoirs, stating "Risk management can never achieve perfection," and that "regulation could not have altered the course."

Factor Seven: Greed is Good, or "Let Them Eat Cake"

> "What kind of society isn't structured on greed? The problem of social organization is how to set up an arrangement under which greed will do the least harm..." — Milton Friedman

Or. as Steven Pearlstein, Pulitzer prize-winning *Washington Post* columnist, says, "Greed is fine, it's stupidity that hurts." Greed is here to stay. It cannot be entirely eliminated from any human enterprise, let alone financial markets which run on two emotions: greed and fear. As Michael Lewis, bestselling author and *New York Times* financial writer says, "You might as well try eliminating lust and envy." Greed is a complicated emotion. In just the right amount, it powerfully fixes one's focus on what's required to succeed. Even the Bible recognizes greed: "All toil and skillful work come from a man's envy of his neighbor." (*Ecclesiastes 4:4*). Lack of greed is why the Soviet Union was so unproductive. But greed, like fear, must be used sparingly. Too much of it, and you are sacrificing long-term prosperity for short-term gain. Way too much of it, and you are seized by it. You will abandon all your principles and moral judgments. At that point you are no better than a junkie looking for the next fix. That this simple truth was, by his own admission, overlooked by Alan Greenspan, the world's biggest money man throughout the period leading to our crisis, speaks as powerfully as anything of the need to regulate greed. If the "The Oracle" (Greenspan's nickname) can't see greed overtaking common sense, who can?

Greed, even to the point of excess and outrageousness, has always been part and parcel of the entrepreneurial culture that drives Wall Street success. But, something happened to warp that culture such that there is no longer any connection between the success and the reward.

Let's give Merrill Lynch CEO, John Thain, the "Marie Antoinette Award" for spending $1.2 million redecorating his office as Rome burned. But that was nothing!

Chapter 3: The Housing Bubble, or "Hell in a Handbasket"

Thain handed out $4 billion in bonuses after the company had already become insolvent and was sold to Bank of America for a fire sale price, and days before he admitted a further $15 billion in losses. Now that's more than greed. It's thievery! In major Wall Street firms, the influence of huge bonuses regardless of performance is a major corrupting influence. Thain had included a $30-40 million bonus for himself, but after the shocked reaction, he agreed to reduce it to $10 million. A nasty letter from New York Attorney General Andrew Cuomo followed, and what he got was zero.

Merrill Lynch lost $27 billion in 2008, almost $16 billion of it in just the last quarter. The reason? Right after the Merrill Lynch/Bank of America merger had been announced and the financial world stood poised on the brink of collapse, Thain thought it would be a good time to aggressively trade high-risk mortgage securities. In his words, he thought "they had bottomed out." Another postcard Cuomo sent Thain was a subpoena to appear and explain the $4 billion in bonuses. Thain's sage explanation for the bonuses (on CNBC) was "If you don't pay your best people you will destroy your franchise, they will go elsewhere." Maureen Dowd, writing for the *Wall St. Journal* counters: "Hello? They destroyed the franchise. Let's call their bluff. Let's see what a great job market it is for the geniuses of capitalism who lost $15 billion in three months and helped usher in socialism."

The Age of Entitlement: How Greed and Arrogance Got Us Here

Bankrupt Lehman Brothers owned a fleet of 12 aircraft, unrivaled in the corporate world. Not just Lear jets either, four of them were Boeing 737s and 767s. Lehman probably had the highest "aircraft capacity to corporate book value" ratio ever! Not to be outdone, Citibank decided to go ahead with a planned $50 million luxury jet purchase, even after getting $85 billion in taxpayer bailout funds. This, even after the auto industry CEOs got roasted for flying into town on their chariots of fire. The "Citiboobs" (as described by the *New York Post*) still didn't get it. The banker aristocracy has no shame. Besides, from their perspective, the world hasn't changed. It's **our** world that has changed. Fortunately, the Obama administration learned about the luxury jet and put the kibosh on it.

No one, even among the general population, really cared what was going on as long their 401Ks were growing. It was all part of how business gets done. When we investors got in trouble, suddenly we started to care. A lot. Suddenly we were seeking friends to hear our tales of injustice. And the surprising thing is that most of us investors never considered we might take a big loss. We believed there were protections in place after the crash of 1929 and "Black Monday," the crash of 1987, to prevent this kind of meltdown. Well, clearly we were wrong.

The ruling paradigm among traders is to trade for the short term. There's often no other reality beyond the next quarter or the year-end bonus, or even today's stock market close. Anyone not maximizing short-term gain, or God forbid,

Chapter 3: The Housing Bubble, or "Hell in a Handbasket"

refusing to participate in irresponsible trading, would be quickly replaced by someone who would. With no accountability or reward for the long-term performance of a stock, why would anyone care what they bought or sold as long they made money **today**? The performance bonuses that traders and management receive reflect only the short-term success of the stock, regardless of the long-term success of the company. If the company tanks next year because of risky trading, these people are not asked to repay their bonuses.

The stock market becomes a casino, with prosperity available only to those with the money and chutzpah to manipulate stocks from one day to the next. It doesn't help to build strong American companies, it only provides companies with an incentive to manipulate their own short-term position in the market. Also, Mom and Pop investors who just want to save for retirement have no chance to succeed in a market that hurtles from one popping bubble to the next.

Similarly, there is no way that Madoff's Ponzi scheme could have been perpetrated all these years without all sorts of people winking and nodding. To inflict this kind of damage, there had to be a massive collective primal shrug by everyone involved at every level. So, it's not that "the system" doesn't work. If works fabulously well, for the fabulously wealthy. And we naively bought a piece of it. Even if we didn't buy a piece of it, even if we kept our money under the mattress, it still affects us.

When tech stocks went bust in 2000, Wall Street's integrity did not bust with it. In fact, the system worked pretty much as designed and corrected an overvaluation of tech stocks. This time it is not a correction, this is a systemic failure at every level, and even if stocks recover one day, Wall Street's brand may not. Reputation, image and confidence are everything. Once people lose confidence, as happened with Lehman Brother and Bear Stearns, there is nothing left.

International markets that once modeled themselves on Wall Street now regard it as a pariah. It may take 10 years for the confidence to return, and it may not ever return. According to Peter Schiff of Euro Pacific Capital, it could mean the rise of new financial capitals around the globe. "Wall Street risks losing its prominence to foreigners just like the auto and textile industries did," Schiff says. "More deals will take place... in places like Hong Kong, Dubai, Shanghai and London. More and more companies will list their shares on other stock markets." Since the crash, Peter Schiff has gained new notoriety for his "spot-on" prediction two years ago of when and how the meltdown would occur. To see an eight-minute video that is chilling in its prescience, log onto YouTube.com and search for "Peter Schiff Was Right 2006-2007 (2nd Edition)."

— Chapter Four —

The Aftermath

> *"Ordinary riches can be stolen; real riches cannot."* — Oscar Wilde

Blame It on Barney Frank?

In the media fallout from the subprime mess, conservative pundits have been quick to blame Barney Frank and the Community Re-investment Act (CRA) for pressuring Fannie Mae and Freddie Mac to issue bad loans. The reasoning goes like this: If Congress didn't force banks to lend to poor and minority borrowers, none of this subprime business would have happened. For this to be true, one would have to believe that people worth hundreds of millions, and companies worth hundreds of billions, were brought to their knees by poor and minority buyers.

The CRA, which was created by Jimmy Carter, has enjoyed wide bi-partisan support despite its recent vilification This act encourages banks to expand home ownership to people previously excluded for racial, ethnic, or sometimes economic reasons. Blaming the CRA for the subprime collapse is just plain wrong. For one thing, the CRA pertains to regular banks, not investment banks. The vast majority of unsound loans were originated by giant mortgage companies and other financial institutions outside the CRA's jurisdiction. Furthermore, a huge portion of the mortgage defaults occurred in luxury properties such as high-end Miami condos. The CRA never suggested irrational lending standards, securitizing the loans into investments, or using insane debt-to-capital ratios.

The best refutation is the "ethical" subprime lending industry, which continues to thrive with default rates of less than 1%. They hold most of their own mortgages and don't sell them into the secondary market. They know they have to live with the loans they extend. These lenders carefully screen clients with subprime credit ratings and charge them a slightly higher rate. The ethical subprime industry is thriving and growing, because these companies turn a good profit while helping to build the communities they serve. One company, the Opportunity Finance Network, lent $2.1 billion in 2007 with .75% charge-offs, even better than the traditional mortgage market! The gimmickry that defined the larger subprime market, like teaser rates, adjustable mortgages with resets, no down payment loans, and no income verification loans, was something the ethical lenders never bought into. These mostly small companies are working in the same neighborhoods as bankrupted giants like Ameriquest, and have outlived the subprime disaster using the same safe business model that made them successful for many years.

Over half of defaulting mortgages that have been renegotiated are still failing. This proves that these particular mortgages should simply never have been written, not that lending money to people with less than stellar credit is impossible. As Daniel Gross of *Newsweek* suggests: "Lending money to poor people is not inherently risky, many decades of initiatives of this type have a proven high repayment rate. On the other hand, lending to extremely rich guys such as Richard Fuld of Lehman Brothers? That can be really risky."

It's Never "Different This Time"

> "Conscience whispers, but interest screams aloud." — J. Petit-Senn

In the stock market run-up to the dot-com boom, market gurus claimed the rules of the game had changed. Traditional indicators of a company's success, like profits, no longer applied. In fact, so many new companies were fighting for market share in this rapidly expanding market, if you were making a profit, you probably weren't growing your company fast enough. Price-to-earnings ratios (the worth of a company relative to its earnings) hit astonishing levels. Companies that had no useful product or service, and no income, were worth more than General Motors. And that was back when General Motors was worth something. The resulting bubble imploded and the fallout is something we are still feeling almost a decade later.

The next mega-bubble would be houses, and it happened astoundingly quickly after the tech bubble burst in 2001. Wall Street did not invent the housing bubble, but wasted no time learning how to inflate it. There were no lessons learned from the dot-com bust, no chastening, there was only the headlong rush into the next bubble. But this was to be no ordinary bubble. The financial mechanisms born of deregulation were in place, along with a new bold attitude of entitlement on Wall Street. They milked short-term profits with little regard to the sustainability of the new bubble.

The housing bubble was built on a foundation of "false prosperity," pointedly described by economist Henry C. K. Liu in his *Open Letter to World Leaders* attending the November 15th 2008 White House Summit on Financial Markets and the World Economy, "... For the last three decades, economists have denied the possibility of another Great Depression like the one that followed the collapse of the speculative bubble created by unfettered US financial markets of the 'Roaring Twenties.' They deluded themselves that false prosperity built on debt could be sustainable with monetary indulgence. Now history is repeating itself, this time with a new, more lethal virus that has infested deregulated global markets with 'innovative' debt securitization, structured finance, and maverick banking operations flush with excess liquidity provided by accommodating central banks. **A massive structure of phantom wealth was built on the quicksand of debt manipulation.** [emphasis added] This debt bubble finally imploded in July 2007 and is now threatening to bring down the entire global financial system and cause an economic meltdown, unless enlightened political leadership adopts coordinated corrective measures on a global scale."

Chapter 4: The Aftermath

Now everyone is looking for the bottom, asking themselves if this is just another business cycle, and, if so, when can we resume business as usual? Long-time critics of the conventional economy suggest the financial system has to be rebuilt from the ground up, but one wonders if any of the current players shaping the bailout really grasp the bigger picture. And, if so, do they have the will to tackle the real underlying issues? Can we rebuild an economy with real value built into it? Can we re-regulate some sanity into the markets? Must the money in capital markets always buy out the morality? It is interesting to note how the bailout plan keeps changing and the forecast for recovery keeps getting pushed back. It appears the plan is to patch the markets back together and limp along to the next boom and bust cycle.

The bailout has the feeling of a "shell game," the goal being to throw money at the problem and then move it around so fast it's impossible to tell if it did any good. The evening news mantra is "don't expect to see the 'bottom' until late 2009." It is more likely we will see the gaping abyss in 2009. The bottom may be nowhere in sight.

The Bailout: Trying to Lose Weight by Loosening Your Belt

> "A billion here and a billion there, and pretty soon you're talking real money." — Everett Dirksen

Sadness surrounds every aspect of the "Bailout." The word needs no introduction, taking the prize as the most "Googled" word of the year. There's a sadness that the general public was so blindsided by market forces driven by greed and short-term gain. A sadness that so many lives are affected by situations so beyond their control; retirement funds and pensions wiped out, thousands of jobs eliminated. Mom and Pop businesses try to survive in a financial climate scrubbed of hope and joy. High school seniors enter higher education with college savings depleted or gone, and college loans impossible to obtain. College graduates enter a workforce rapidly shedding workers of every description. Millions of people lose their homes, regardless of whether they should have known they couldn't afford them. The saddest thing for all of these people is to watch money being channeled to the very people who caused the mess. What's worse is the pervasive feeling that the whole effort to jumpstart the economy has by all accounts been a complete flop.

Chapter 4: The Aftermath

Treasury Secretary Henry Paulson said taxpayers would be kept in the loop about the billions being given out. "We need oversight," he said. "We need transparency. I want it. We all want it." That's not exactly the way it has played out.

From the very beginning, the sputtering start to the bailout was all over the map, the target of the bailout changing from one day to the next, frightening Wall Street and anyone else who was paying attention. One minute the government was buying toxic assets from investment houses, next they were pressuring banks to take money some didn't even want, all in an effort to force-feed the credit supply. Even then, businesses that rely on credit were going under. Banks were not using the money for loans, but instead kept the money to improve their balance sheets, and to acquire other more precariously balanced banks.

The financial blogs featured mocking headlines like "Moving on to Plan B: there is no Plan B." Neither Paulson nor Bernanke had an alternate plan to rebuild stable financial markets on something other than low-interest rates and whacky financial deals. It seemed the whole thing was being invented on the fly.

The Congressional Oversight Panel hastily assembled to oversee the bailout was still without phones or fax machines at the end of December 2008. By that time $350 billion had been doled out to God knows who, by Neel Kashkari, a 35-year-old banker six years out of business school in charge of the doling. Far from the transparency promised at the outset, the Fed refused to divulge the bailout recipients for fear there would be runs on those banks.

With the public and most of the press focused on the reported $700 billion bailout, *Bloomberg News* began quietly calculating the real costs associated with the bill, piecing together the real story from economists, academic researchers and interviews with Fed and FDIC officials. The truth is that taxpayers will be saddled with almost $7.7 trillion if the Fed fulfills just the existing pledges and loan guarantees. Fool.com, the popular financial website, puts the total even higher, at $8.6 trillion! It will be the single largest expenditure in US history, half the size of our entire 2008 economy last year, or twice what we spent (in inflation-adjusted dollars) fighting WWII. Congress and the press are not even talking about this part of the bailout, (the loan guarantees the Fed has made), which are shrouded in mystery.

According to ABC's John Stossel, even some of the bailout's original supporters, like Barney Frank, (D-MA) the chairman of the committee that approved the plan, are withdrawing their support. "Because we've been dissatisfied with the way in which they've spent the first half of this, we have blocked them from spending the second half," Frank said. Other lawmakers had more pointed comments: Representative Carolyn Malone, (D-NY), called it a "dismal failure." Representative Virginia Brown-Waite, (R-FL) declared "we are going down a rat-hole." Congress moved to

Chapter 4: The Aftermath

withhold the second half of the bailout to be resolved by the Obama administration.

The Fed claims that all pledges are backed by collateral, but will not identify what that collateral is. Elizabeth Warren (head of the Congressional Oversight Panel that doesn't have phones yet) says, "We don't even know, in the case of the Fed, to which institutions it's going, much less to what use it's being put."

The government is pretending that the collateral being offered to secure the loans has some value. This then begs the question, "If this collateral is actually worth something, why don't private investors want it, at any price?" "These questions are just baffling," says Barney Frank. The same news story quotes Daniel Mitchell of the Cato Institute, "We don't know what banks are going to the Fed, we don't know what collateral they're offering, and the politicians and bureaucrats are telling us it's for our own good, because if we actually know the truth, we won't be able to handle it, or we'll have a run on the bank... this is what you find with corrupt third-world governments and yet we're going down that same path of the rule of law being set aside..."

For those steeped in the consumption model, the theory that another wild spending spree will cure everything, a stimulus package to jump-start spending seems reasonable. But that underestimates the deep level of consumer retrenchment. For the first time since records were kept (1952), US households have begun to pay down their debt. In an economy which depends on consumer spending for 72% of the GDP, with a million jobs lost every eight weeks, a check for $600 does not even come close to cutting it. Not when the consumer psyche is hanging by a thread for fear of destitution. The idea that the consumption bubble can be re-inflated is just plain retrograde thinking. If you've got some money, for God's sake hang onto it! You will need it to buy the necessities of life.

Ironically, the stimulus plan that was presented by the Obama administration, with zero Republican support, was not that different from what Republicans proposed in Fall 2008. Clearly neither party has learned to play nice. No one is reaching across the aisle, which is what the American people want. That alone would give America some confidence. Most economists agree some sort of stimulus is needed, but that's where the agreement ends. In truth, no one really knows what will work because we haven't been here before. But, one thing is certain. If we hadn't foolishly accumulated a mountain of debt during the good times, we wouldn't be quite so broke now.

Blogger Mike Whitney describes the bailout as "trying to inflate a truck tire with a turkey baster," and declares this "the point where monetary policy and lunacy intersect." Whitney compares Ben Bernanke's plan, the Fed buying its own US treasuries to keep interest rates low, to "trying to cover a bank overdraft by issuing a check to one's self."

Chapter 4: The Aftermath

The original crux of the bailout, buying "toxic assets" (or as Paul Krugman calls them, "cash for trash") to take them off the books of struggling companies, had some obvious problems. The reason the assets were toxic was because they had little or no value, and, in fact, couldn't even be valued because no one wanted them. The Wall Street wizards don't exactly have the best track record for asset valuation. Crafting a deal to buy an asset of undetermined value, and saddling taxpayers with ownership of these questionable assets proved so unpopular, Paulson and company scrubbed the effort.

The new "plan," cash infusions with no strings attached, given to whichever large endangered corporations asked (or didn't ask or even want), failed to instill confidence in anyone. "Joe" (not the plumber) on the street sees companies like Citibank receive billions of dollars (a total of $85 billion so far), when they just reset Joe's credit card from 6% to 30% because a payment was one day late. Or because they intentionally changed the due date without notice. Joe also knows people who are losing their houses. Maybe it was personal mismanagement, or maybe it was subterfuge by fast-talking mortgage sharks. Don't expect Joe to ever think it's fair. He's been busy living an honest life while rich high-flying financiers were ruining the economy. And ruining Joe's life.

Even though the cash infusions to banks are meant to prevent an irreversible meltdown, the bailout has never been presented as a necessary sacrifice. Most Americans have never had to make a huge sacrifice, certainly not *en masse*, and they are in no mood to start now. This is especially difficult because average people who live by the rules are expected to help white-collar criminals walk away with golden parachutes. Help for those hurting most is nowhere in sight.

While the bailouts to banks were immediate, help for struggling mortgage holders was miniscule and a long time coming. Congress mandated some mortgage help in the original bailout, but Paulson refused to comply. Some banks had programs in place, but a substantial mortgage relief program didn't happen until late February 2009, and even then, was not a large-scale plan. Deciding who deserves mortgage help and how to provide it is tricky at best. But forestalling additional foreclosures will lessen the impact of more mortgage investments going bad, and more importantly, will free up money at the bottom of the system instead of just the top.

In October of 2008, Paulson was managing the "mother of all bailouts" in a manner that seemed reckless, secretive, and arbitrary; bordering on an outright swindle to benefit his Wall Street cronies. The text of the bailout plan was downright scary. "Decisions by the Secretary pursuant to the authority of this Act are non-reviewable and committed to agency discretion, and may not be reviewed by any court of law or any administrative agency." Paulson had a dismal record on spotting trouble, and played a large role in creating it. Here is Mr. Paulson, quoted by *The Associated Press*, on July 20, 2008: "It's a safe banking system, a

Chapter 4: The Aftermath

sound banking system. Our regulators are on top of it. This is a very manageable situation." Why should we have trusted his private and secretive discretion in doling out billions to failing companies? There were few economists with any faith in the principles behind the plan, let alone its method of implementation.

Even Congress was freaked out at the way Paulson was conducting the bailout in the last days of the Bush administration, and halted the release of the second half. That task fell to Obama's new Treasury Secretary, Timothy Geithner, and he did not inspire anyone expecting "change." Coming straight from chairmanship of the New York Fed branch, Geithner was supposedly the "point man" responsible for Wall Street activities, and was also the architect of the now widely-reviled AIG bailout plan. It was just another promotion in the "good old boy" network, and not one that was earned.

Bailout plan Part II was released with much fanfare in mid-February 2009. To say it was a colossal flop is putting a positive spin on its reception: the Dow fell almost 400 points. Perhaps the criticism that it "lacked specifics" was unfair considering that Bailout Part I lacked any specifics whatsoever.

The financial blogs dubbed this new plan "Washington happy talk." A recycled collection of measures which haven't worked in the past, re-packaged with those fancy new acronyms people are so fond of. It amounted to more of the same: propping up banks by using taxpayer money to buy lousy assets at inflated prices. Entitled thinking led Wall Street to believe it could endlessly leverage wealth with no consequences. Now there is a refusal to accept the painful correction that must follow.

All of these bailout activities, in fact everything done by the Fed, the Treasury and the SEC, seems geared toward "mission #1," propping up stock prices. Confidence in the integrity of the markets will never recover with the government injecting fake value. The Stock Market itself, not the government, is meant to be the final arbiter of a company's value, and should be left to clean its own house.

Selecting specific banks to bail out sends the markets a message that those banks won't fail, that Uncle Sam will do whatever is necessary for them to survive. That has the unfortunate side-effect of making non-bailed-out banks into pariahs, even though they may have played it safe and remain relatively healthy.

Because there is no confidence anywhere, no one knows how healthy any bank really is, which makes only the failed bailed-out banks safe to deal with. It has made life more difficult for banks that behaved, because they get frozen out of the credit market. This phenomenon illustrates the dangers of introducing Socialist-type micro-controls into free markets. The Law of Unintended Consequences will take you places you never wanted to go.

Chapter 4: The Aftermath

Giving money to banks with no strings attached gives them a *de facto* government stamp of approval, the best insurance a bank could buy. What's more, the bank doesn't have to buy the insurance, they're actually paid to take it. In addition, taxpayers will be on the hook for whatever future funds are needed to keep these "chosen" banks solvent.

The injection of money to banks to provide the liquidity to lend was sold on false premises. Liquidity in the credit markets didn't happen. The real purpose was to make the government into Wall Street's insurance carrier, and to reimburse wealthy investors for their lost equity. In the words of Naomi Klein, writing for *The Nation*, this was "a safety net for the people who need it least, subsidized by the people who need it most."

A sure sign that banks are still delusional is their push to eliminate "mark-to-market" accounting standards. This would allow banks to record the value of their assets as what they paid for them, not what they are really worth in the market. The lobbying for this is intense, and regulators are very close to caving. Imagine if mortgage holders could do that!

In the words of blogger Mike Whitney: "The investor class has rejiggered the system to meet their particular needs. Financial wizardry has replaced factories, capital formation and hard assets while real wealth has been replaced by chopped up bits of mortgage paper, stitched together by Ivy League MBAs, and sold to investors as priceless gemstones. This is the system that Bernanke is trying to resuscitate with his multi-trillion dollar injections; a system that shifts a larger and larger amount of the nation's wealth to a smaller and smaller group of elites."

The great and powerful engines that drove prosperity for many years, like mortgage-backed securities and home equity loans, have not just slowed down. They have virtually ceased to exist. The volume of debt issued worldwide plunged by 75% in the last three months of 2008. Pouring liquidity into the markets has not eased credit because it hasn't addressed any of the underlying causes, which have more to do with a loss of confidence than the amount of money available to lend. How can there be any confidence when fraud, predatory lending, ratings manipulation, and other white collar crimes go unpunished? The largest financial swindle of all time has seen not one indictment. Possibly because in a market almost completely deregulated, almost everything is legal.

How can there be any confidence when there is no day of reckoning for failed business models? From the most powerful hedge fund trader to the simplest homeowner, there is no reason to believe anything in the markets will work as advertised. We are seeing a financial order stripped of order. In a system where confidence is the grease that lubricates every transaction, the loss of it has caused the entire machinery to grind to a screeching halt. There is no pool of speculators willing to risk their capital, because lack of market discipline removes the foundation of every investor's decision to part with their cash.

Chapter 4: The Aftermath

For confidence to be restored, the system would need to be rebuilt from the ground up. The confidence would have to come from something people could believe in. Many think it would have to be done the hard way, by letting the creative chaos of the marketplace kill off the weakest companies, no matter how large they are. Few can argue that when government rewards the incompetence of fools by letting them live to trade another day, a viral infection comes imbedded in whatever limited recovery is forced to happen. The sacrifice required by letting the building burn to the ground and rebuilding from the ashes is just too difficult for the entitled generation.

How will the financial landscape be re-arranged? An automotive expert commenting on industry changes to come predicted that out of 65 car-makers worldwide today, only five will survive, possibly none of them US companies. That is a world we cannot comprehend. Letting the system detoxify itself by natural selection may seem too cruel to contemplate. But artificially re-ordering a financial mess decades in the making will require almost Soviet-style economic engineering. Engineering that would undermine or even kill the entrepreneurial spirit at the heart of a dynamic economy. Even more scary: the tinkering would be done by the same geniuses who made the mess in the first place.

Unfortunately, President Obama's financial team is comprised almost entirely of people who rose up through the status quo, and some of them, like Geithner and Summers, are directly responsible for helping to create the conditions that led us here.

Japan's "lost decade" saw multiple stimulus and bailout packages fail to restart their economy, and only when the banks were finally forced to acknowledge their losses did their economy somewhat recover. Twenty-five years later, the Nikkei has still not made up for lost ground.

Case in point is AIG, the failed insurance giant that was deemed too important to the world economy to fail. Three bailouts and $150 billion later, AIG was in even worse shape. AIG promised to repay the bailout by selling its divisions that are still performing, but so far has sold only $2.2 billion of assets, and doesn't have much left to sell that anyone wants to buy. There are bidders for AIG's and others' bad assets, but the bids are so low, they are not being accepted, even though they need the money. Why would they if Uncle Sam is coming to the rescue? On March 1, 2009, AIG posted the largest quarterly loss in US history, $61.8 billion, and the Fed stepped in with its fourth bailout of $30 billion, for a total of $180 billion. The government now owns a shell that the stock market gives little value to. AIG's remaining assets are worth only a fraction of what it owes. It's essentially been bankrupt for quite a while, but is being kept alive as a "zombie" company with no hope of ever repaying its debts.

Same for Citicorp, or should we call it "Citi-corpse"? After multiple bailouts, still on life-support. This is exactly what our own experts advised Japan against. But Japan couldn't accept the pain, and neither will we.

Chapter 4: The Aftermath

The bailout is a hugely expensive shot in the dark being engineered behind closed doors by the very people responsible for setting up the framework for the collapse. But this may not be the worst part. It may not even be that the entire bailout is going to banks and fat cats, with none of it going to restore the pension funds and 401Ks that we normal people hoped to retire on. What's most disturbing is that the bailout is morally wrong in so many ways. It sends the wrong message about personal responsibility. It forces people who acted responsibly to pay for those who didn't. It allows the perpetrators to benefit from their abuse of the system. And, aside from these ethical considerations, the bailout transfers the risk of falling markets from the banks to the American taxpayer.

It's a world gone mad with entitlement mentality. On Wall Street you have speculators creating a money machine built on debt manipulation, a machine capable of enormous profits, but not capable of surviving itself. To add the ultimate insult to injury, the economic collapse of the free world did not prevent many of the companies extorting taxpayers' bailout money from handing themselves tens of billions in year-end bonuses.

On Pennsylvania Avenue, you have generations of lawmakers completely ignoring the building mountain of debt, giving little thought to how the future economy can function with such a burden. Instead of reducing this debt or even just limiting it, they enact tax cuts, spending increases, and huge new entitlement programs. Rebate checks are issued with borrowed money. In the saddest display of entitlement, we see a $700 billion bailout bill opposed by 78% of the people, that the House wouldn't pass without $100 billion in additional tax cuts and earmark spending. I wish I were kidding, but one of the earmarks added to this bill was a subsidy on wooden toy arrows.

On Main Street, you have homeowners with maxed-out credit cards and no savings buying Escalades with home equity loans. Somehow, the last generation that tried to change the world, the Woodstock generation, became the SUV generation. Then came the "me" and "X" and "Y" generations. The official "entitlement" generation (born between 1979–1994) fits in there somewhere. All these people are us, the people that will not elect a politician from either party who doesn't offer a tax cut, who dares speak of any meaningful sacrifice that would prevent the next generation from inheriting a bankrupt nation.

In truth, we increased the deficit to completely unsustainable levels before we needed these bailouts and stimulus packages. We seem determined to discover just when the rest of the world will declare the US derelict, unable to pay its bills. Or, when will we reach the tipping point of "third-world type" hyperinflation caused by printing too much money. World history is rife with the economies of countries that are declared "basket cases" because of these two things. With the arrogance afforded only by superpowers, we think that it can't happen here.

Chapter 4: The Aftermath

Modified Limited Hangout

> "All media exist to invest our lives with artificial perceptions and arbitrary values." — Marshall McLuhan

Throughout the economic turmoil, as in war, the biggest casualty was the truth. The real extent of the economic devastation has been on a "need to know" basis. Some financial prognosticators claim that Citibank is bankrupt even after the $85 billion bailout. They're just waiting for the right time to tell us. The market plunge following the fall of Lehman Brothers proved the system cannot absorb another big shock. Better to bleed the taxpayers and prop up a zombie bank. In early March 2009, the plunging market rebounded after Citibank reported a profit of $8 billion for the first two months of the year. Nowhere did that news story mention that was an "operating profit." The ledger still has two sides. Put that operating profit against the hundreds of billions in losses, and the trillions in "off-books" risky exposure that's still hanging out there, and the picture remains dismal at best.

The government's attempt to put the best spin on bad news may be intended to calm the public, but it's reminiscent of a CIA method described by Richard Helms in his book, *The Man Who Kept Secrets*. It's called "modified limited hangout." The "hangout" part is letting the truth hang out there in the wind for all to see, when the situation is so bad and so obvious, it's staring everyone in the face. The "limited" is: don't tell them the whole truth. The "modified" is: put a positive spin on what you do tell them.

Fortunately, we now have a "blogosphere" of inquisitive, interconnected individuals to dissect the "truth." The truth is out there! When Jon Stewart on Comedy Central becomes the first media personality to go after Wall Street with hard-hitting journalism, journalism has a problem.

Paul B. Ferrell of the *Wall Street Journal*, one of the few to accurately predict the dot-com bust right at its peak, has compiled a list of reasons why we are far from the bottom of this bubble. In his June 2, 2008 article called *20 Reasons New Megabubble Pops in 2011*, he claims "Greed blinded us to the subprime meltdown and it'll blind us next time too." Some of Ferrell's observations include former Fed governor, Ed Gramlich, warning Greenspan of the coming subprime crisis in 2000. Ferrell also notes Peter Peterson, Nixon's Secretary of Commerce, declaring in his 2004 book, *Running on Empty*, "This administration and the Republican Congress have presided over the biggest, most reckless deterioration of America's finances in history, creating a "bankrupt nation." The article in its entirety makes for scintillating reading, especially if you follow it up with his updated November 19, 2008 article, *30 Reasons for Great Depression 2 by 2011*.

A timely example of criminal fraud flourishing in an atmosphere of deregulated greed was provided by the Bernard Madoff scandal, where the world's largest hedge fund turned out to be a $50 billion dollar Ponzi scheme.

Chapter 4: The Aftermath

While the headline news stories featured the grizzly aftermath of wiped-out endowments, charities and investors, the back story revealed just one more tiring tale of fraud committed in plain view of regulators over a long period of time. The Securities and Exchange Commission was repeatedly alerted to Madoff's numbers being wacky. They didn't add up; you just couldn't make the math work.

One such private citizen investigator was Harry Markopolos, a Massachusetts accountant who spent seven years documenting the whole affair, and sending the information to the SEC. In 2005, Harry even supplied the SEC with a 17-page documented "roadmap," entitled *The World's Largest Hedge Fund Is a Fraud*, which was simultaneously published in the *Wall St. Journal*. The SEC never took it seriously, and Madoff was finally turned in by his two sons after confessing to them. Madoff's fund was the only hedge fund in existence that refused to allow outside audits. Apparently that was not enough to alarm its many investors, who were satisfied with the steady double digit returns that many others thought impossible.

It comes as no surprise that this trail leads straight to Washington. The Madofff family has a long history of using multiple methods to direct huge amounts of lobbyist money toward beltway politicians, and agencies in charge of Wall Street regulatory bodies, including the SEC and others. In fact, Madoff was involved in a similar scheme in Florida in the 1960s where two accountants were charged with fraudulently raising over $440 million for Madoff.

The Age of Entitlement: How Greed and Arrogance Got Us Here

The accountants were charged, but Madoff was never fingered. Representing the accountants in that matter was Ira Lee Sorkin, the former head of SEC New York City region. Sorkin represents Madoff today, and the same trustee named to sort out the mess in the 60s has been named as trustee of funds in the current matter. But wait, that's not all! Mark Mukasy, son of the Bush's Attorney General, was representing a key Madoff employee, resulting in the highest law enforcement officer in the nation recusing himself from the investigation of the largest Ponzi scheme in history.

As for the SEC, the Madoff scandal exposes their real role: to protect politically-connected financial predators from investors, instead of the other way around. Markopolis was not the only whistleblower. Goldman Sachs was so suspicious of Madoff they would not do business with him. There is a *quid pro quo* between the SEC and Wall Street, a well-worn path of SEC Directors going on to lucrative Wall Street careers.

Chapter 4: The Aftermath

"Too Big to Fail" Means Too Big to Exist

> "If there are men in this country big enough to own the government of the United States, they are going to own it."
> — Woodrow Wilson, 1913

There is a simple reason that "anti-trust" has been a primary concern of economists since the age of "robber barons" in the 1800's. Market dominance kills competition. The larger a corporation gets, the more they can behave in a monopolistic fashion. Once they dominate a region, they are able to ride roughshod over local political interests, demanding tax breaks and zoning variances. When they dominate nationally and own a large chunk of the GNP, their political clout allows them to set the national agenda. They are now beyond the control of regulators and can behave in any manner they please, even if it is destructive. Even if it is self-destructive.

Growth is not necessarily bad. If a company's growth comes from inside the company itself, it means someone valued their product or service. But if growth came by acquisitions, there is no guarantee that the resulting larger enterprise has any greater value beyond some CEO's dreams (or delusions) of grandeur.

Bigness is fundamentally bad for everyone. Limited competition always means higher prices for the consumer. Local individualized service goes out the window, and small but profitable "Mom and Pop" companies are driven out by large inefficient conglomerates. But that's just the beginning. When companies are smaller, the marketplace decides which of them live or die. Losing the bad ones enhances the efficiencies of the ones that are left. When a bunch of smaller companies become a bumbling colossus with many parts, some efficient and some not, capitalism cannot function as intended. If General Motors broke up into six or seven parts, some of them would actually survive. When a corporation is so big that its failure is a national catastrophe requiring taxpayer rescue, it becomes legalized extortion.

Citigroup attempted to become a one-stop financial "supermarket," providing not only banking services, but insurance, credit cards, securities trading and derivatives as well. When this enterprise started failing it was so big no one could buy it, and no one even wanted it, even at $2 a share. The government gave them $85 billion to prevent them from failing, but that disguises the fact that they had already failed. The share price says that. Now Citigroup is frantically trying to break itself up, and sell the pieces that still have some value. But the financial blogs say that Citigroup still has a trillion dollars in toxic assets that are "off the books," and that the government is keeping the true financial condition secret. Many banks probably have losses so deep that their equity is wiped out. It's not a case of protecting these banks from failure for the good of the taxpayer. These banks are already insolvent and will now take the taxpayer down with them. "The bailout" is nothing more than the financial elite protecting its own.

So far there is no indication that Government or the bailout experts get the "too big to fail" thing yet. The four biggest banks in the US, J.P. Morgan Chase, Citigroup, Bank of America, and Wells Fargo, still possess 64 percent of the assets of US commercial banks. The sell-offs that have occurred are more like shuffling the deck from the top than a profound realization that "big" is bad. Take for example the plan to graft failing unsalvageable financial institutions onto stronger retail banks. Working great so far, isn't it? Previously healthy Bank of America (stock now down 65%) required a bailout following indigestion from absorbing hideously debt-laden Merrill Lynch and mortgage lender, Countrywide.

We can only hope regulators will prevent corporate America from becoming so powerful that fundamental capitalist principles are undermined. The founding fathers imagined an America that was not ruled by robber barons. A country where the hard work of an honest person cannot be so easily torn asunder by the foolish greed of a wealthy elite.

— Chapter Five —

Bubblenomics

800-Pound Gorillas: Social Security and Medicare

> "After 215 years of trying, we have finally discovered a special interest group that includes 100 percent of the population. Now we can vote ourselves rich." — P.J. O'Rourke

It's been said that if you really want to keep a secret, hide it in plain sight. No truer example exists than the unfunded future liabilities of Social Security and Medicare/Medicaid. They potentially represent our financial ruin. After decades of debate, there's been no action that would alter this picture in any way. It wasn't even mentioned as an issue in the 2008 election by the press, public, or candidates.

In a world where reality counted for something, these future costs would be funded like any other type of insurance, with premiums paid by people in the present, held in trust to be used in the future. Unfortunately, these revenues have been used for years to pay the daily bills of government. The first Baby Boomers have already begun to retire, and as of 2017 the system will start to take in less money than it pays out. Without drastic changes, the system becomes insolvent in 2030.

The Social Security payments now used (or misused) to augment general revenue disguise the true enormity of the deficit. Within a relatively short time, Social Security will eclipse all other costs of government and send an already spiraling deficit out of control into system overload. There have been only five balanced budgets in the last 40 years (all in the Clinton years), but if you remove taxpayer Social Security payments, which should have been saved for future expenditures, the deficit curve has been taking a nosedive for some time, and will become much worse for the rest of this century.

Some think we could solve our financial problems by eliminating fraud, waste and abuse. Or, we could cancel the tax cuts, or end the war in Iraq. These items currently represent about 14% of the budget; helpful, but not even close to covering the shortfall. Other optimists project sufficient future growth to keep the system solvent well into the middle of the century. The United States General Accounting office (GAO) cannot be counted among these optimists. An April 2008 GAO update states "Our updated simulations continue to illustrate that the long-term fiscal outlook is unsustainable." An estimated 80 million Americans will become eligible for retirement benefits in the next two decades, an average of more than 10,000 per day. According to the report, the system faces "...large and growing structural deficits driven primarily by rising health care costs and known demographic trends."

Chapter 5: Bubblenomics

Our government liabilities, including the national debt and the unfunded future costs for Social Security, Medicare, and Medicaid, will soon exceed $60 trillion and are projected to consume 100% of the federal budget by 2030. Of this amount, we have none. By the time today's college graduates retire, the federal government will be out of business unless federal taxes are doubled or benefits are drastically cut.

Judd Gregg (R-NH) speaks on this issue: "The only issue that's more severe than this would be the idea that an Islamic fundamentalist would get his hands on a nuclear weapon and use it against us. Beyond that there is nothing more severe than this. This issue represents the potential fiscal meltdown of this nation, and it absolutely guarantees that our children will have less of a quality of life than we have had. They will have a government they cannot afford, and we will be demanding so much money from them for taxes that they will not have the money to send their kids to college, buy a home or just live a good quality of life."

When the deficit is expressed as a percentage of Gross Domestic Production (GDP), the deficit trend can be tracked through history, as this equation automatically accounts for inflation and other time-specific economic anomalies. The deficit has soared at times throughout history, usually in times of war or fiscal calamity as during the Revolutionary War (40% of GDP), the Civil War (33% of GDP), the Great Depression (44% of GDP), World War II (a whopping 122% of GDP), and the Vietnam War (47% of

GDP). Between these times of soaring deficits, governments made half-hearted efforts to pay down the debt, but the only time the deficit has ever been paid down completely, although briefly, was in 1835 when Andrew Jackson dissolved the Central Bank, withdrew the government's money and paid off the national debt.

The budget deficits of the Reagan years (56% of GDP) can be partially attributed to fighting the Cold War, although the "Reaganomics" tax cuts provided by far the biggest hike to the deficit. George H. W. Bush decried Reagan's "supply-side" theories as "voodoo economics," but tax cuts had already become an entitlement that conservative America demanded, and Bush continued those tax cuts. Soon fiscal reality faced the elder Bush and he was forced to raise taxes. The "no new taxes" mantra came back to haunt him and ultimately cost him his second term. When he left office, the deficit was $4 trillion (64% of GDP).

The Clinton years provided a far more balanced approach to revenues and expenditures. The huge boost in revenues provided by the dot-com boom, however, played the largest part in the first "balanced" budgets in living memory. In reality, the deficit was reduced only slightly (57% of GDP) and if the pilfered Social Security money is properly deducted, the budgets were far from balanced.

The ruling paradigm during the "W" years was more tax cuts, although defining this era as "mainstream conservative economics" proves enigmatic. Somehow fiscal conservatives, who for generations demanded smaller

Chapter 5: Bubblenomics

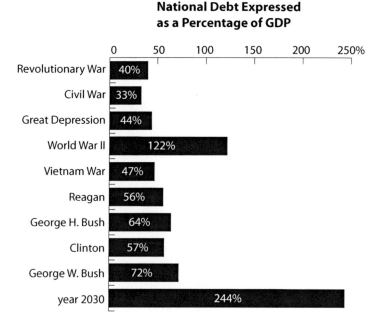

government and tax cuts, seemed to embrace tax cuts without corresponding spending cuts.

As a result, for the first time in history, the deficit soared during a time of relative peace and prosperity. By 2008, even without the bailout costs, the deficit stood at $8.7 trillion (72% of GDP) and, with bailout costs will soon be $10 trillion and counting. The sum of all the deficits rolled forward throughout American history has been doubled in eight short years. The Iraq war and other 9/11-related security costs cannot even begin to account for those increases in spending. Because six of those eight years featured a Republican Congress and a Republican President, (the first President in modern history to never veto a spending bill), and the last two years of Democratic control featured only a tiny majority, this sorry chapter is inescapably owned by the Republicans. The cliché of "tax and spend liberals" had been upended by the "tax cut and spend" conservatives.

The tax cut imperative was so imbedded in the Republican party psyche that in 2002, Secretary of the Treasury, Paul O'Neil, was forced to resign for refusing to support another tax cut. According to O'Neil's own account of his conversation with Cheney at the time, Cheney said "we don't worry about deficits." O'Neil was shocked, and commented later "we need to look at the fate of other countries that have lived beyond their means for a long time, you inevitably get into trouble. When you get extended to the point where you can't service your debt, you're finished."

Twenty years from now, our debt to GDP ratio could be 244%, twice the WWII level. Who is going to lend us money then? In 2007, foreigners (mostly China) bankrolled 75% of our debt. There is no guarantee they will continue to do so. China's Premier has recently stated that he is getting "nervous" about the US debt China holds.

In late February 2009, a group of the nation's top budget analysts warned President Obama that these dire consequences may be close at hand. A worldwide economic downturn, combined with loss of confidence in the ability of the US to pay its debts, may soon make it much harder (and more expensive) for the US to fund its deficits.

The *General Accounting Office April 2008 Report* suggested a series of scenarios that would alleviate the impact of runaway Social Security obligations by taking action immediately. The report stresses "the longer action is delayed, the greater the risk that the eventual changes will be disruptive and destabilizing." Unfortunately, there is no political will for any of these fixes, raising taxes and/or reducing Social Security, Medicaid and Medicare benefits. And now, when many facing retirement have seen their 401Ks decimated, is the worst possible time to tell Americans they must accept reduced retirement payments.

Few politicians dare to state the obvious. One of the few is Congressman Paul Ryan (R-WI) who has offered a measured proposal that addresses these entitlements in a fiscally sustainable manner. His proposal has received little attention on Capitol Hill. A May 2008 Wall Street Journal opinion piece outlining Ryan's proposal received not a single comment letter. Congress's chilly reception was no better; it involves sacrifices not palatable to voters.

Some have said we get the government we deserve, and because there's little appetite in either party for promoting public sacrifice to spare future generations the burden of our obligations, we are indeed are own worst enemy. More accurately, our children's worst enemy.

We should not forget the most disturbing aspect of this entire debate. These obligations are not really "unfunded." The funds for these "entitlements" have been paid for by FICA withholdings from millions of people over a great many years. The money collected was not held in trust; it was used for current budgetary obligations. Treasury "IOUs" were deposited in the Social Security accounts. It is the IOUs that will bankrupt future generations, not the obligations themselves. We spent the money many of us will rely on for retirement for the instant gratification of existing government programs.

"Entitlement," in this instance, is the word used to describe obligations which were bought and paid for by taxpayers. But it really describes the inexplicable greed of politicians who felt entitled to use money that did not belong to them for their own selfish purposes. "Entitlement" also describes the voters who re-elected them. After all, the Social Security deficit is an issue widely known for decades, but almost never discussed in the media or any other public forum. The public may have believed the Social Security money would be repaid like any other loan, but no one, it seems, had any intention of doing so. And no one really wanted to push the issue.

Chapter 5: Bubblenomics

Future Bubbles: Credit Card Debt and Commercial Retail Debt

> "You want 21 percent risk-free? Pay off your credit cards."
> — Andrew Tobias

If you only use credit cards for convenience, airline miles or other rewards, and you pay off your balance every month, the credit card industry sees you as a "deadbeat." Why? Because they make very little money from you. If, on the other hand, you are one of America's 115 million "revolvers" and carry a balance forward each month, you are generating the $30 billion profit the credit card industry enjoyed last year. You are the "sweet spot" of the industry, the focus of all of its marketing; you are the target of rooms full of MBAs who craft the small print of deceptive offers that attract and addict Americans to a debt they can't pay off.

The 650 million credit cards in circulation are creating a new $1.2 trillion debt bubble that could eclipse the housing bubble. While the dollar value of credit card debt does not come close to that of mortgage debt, it is a debt that reaches more widely across society. It is particularly dangerous to those with the least capacity to pay the debt.

Last year, card issuers wrote off $41 billion in unrecoverable debt, this year it will be more than twice that. While subprime mortgage buyers were 11% of the mortgage market, risky borrowers account for something like 30% of outstanding credit card debt. Some companies like

Washington Mutual had 45% of their credit customers in the risky category. Even more affluent American Express customers are falling so far behind that AMEX is seeing their rotten debt double each year.

Another factor that could cause consumer debt to grow exponentially is the end of home equity lending, which represented a huge portion of consumer debt. Once homeowners can no longer tap rising home equity to finance lifestyles they can't afford, it is likely they will use credit cards to stay afloat.

As consumer spending evaporates, retailers are bound to experience massive failures. The last decade has seen a huge national surge in retail mall building. In some areas, over 10% of the retail space is in stores still under construction. By the end of 2008, the number of larger retailers closing stores or shutting down entirely was staggering, but the shock of recession had just started moving through the system. With the availability of cheap capital, increased retail square footage diluted sales dollars and reduced individual store profitability. Many malls have co-tenancy agreements that will cause these malls to cease operation once the anchor store leaves. Some industry analysts predict that 20-25% of retail mall store locations will close in the next 18-24 months. The expected commercial bubble may dwarf the housing bubble.

Chapter 5: Bubblenomics

The Commercial Real Estate Debt Index had already started to plummet on reports of insolvency in several large malls, and derivatives that cover commercial debt were at record levels, but that's just the tip of the iceberg. In the next three years, $530 billion of commercial debt will come due in an atmosphere of frozen credit, and the industry is already standing in line for bailouts with banks, credit card issuers and car companies.

Those Who Fall Through the Cracks

> *"They say it is better to be poor and happy than rich and miserable, but how about a compromise like moderately rich and just moody?"*
> — Princess Diana

American politics has rarely been more stratified than today. Recent elections have been a more vindictive battle than an honest and open public discourse. Republicans and Democrats lock horns over almost everything, but few topics are debated more vigorously than the "social safety net." The prevailing conservative sentiment is that public assistance programs are misguided liberal attempts at social engineering; that the productive members of society are being asked to subsidize lazy individuals waiting for a handout.

Clearly, not everyone has the same economic vigor. In fact, the economy depends on people at every financial level. Some struggling to succeed will benefit from help, some will never thrive and will abuse the help. Overall, though, it stands to reason that the fewer people at the lowest levels falling through the cracks, the better the society. The amount of money legitimately spent to help the poor are not the entitlements that are breaking the bank. The risk/reward link that makes free enterprise work is not endangered by helping people at the bottom of the ladder. Using aid programs to stabilize weaker individuals in any society is not just blind virtue, it is enlightened self-interest. It simply makes the world a more pleasant place to live for everyone. As Parker Palmer says: "Societies' greatness is not to be measured by how well the strongest in its midst can do, but by how well it takes care of the weakest in its midst."

Hard work and improving one's lot in life has its own reward, and lingering bitterness that recipients of aid programs are getting something for nothing is counterproductive, negative thinking. It's reasonable that aid programs should have limits and incentives. Yet some will respond to incentives, while others never will. That doesn't negate the importance of aid programs in keeping the working poor from becoming the desperately poor, and the desperately poor from falling through the cracks altogether. Entitlements programs that accomplish this should be separated from entitlements that people could do without but have come to expect.

Chapter 5: Bubblenomics

As compared with other industrialized nations, we have higher infant mortality, below-average life expectancy, higher rate of medical errors, the largest percentage of medically uninsured. Yet costs in the US are 50% higher than any nation on earth.

Conservatives seem convinced that a government-run health system would be even more expensive, but that hasn't proven true in dozens of other countries. Single-payer, government-run health care is being provided affordably in every industrial nation on earth, except ours. There are compromises, like waiting times for elective surgery, but they are acceptable compromises compared to 40 million people with substandard health care. We are already funding the uninsured through higher medical premiums for people that do have insurance, with much of this care provided by expensive emergency room care.

Instead of providing a comprehensive minimum social safety net for the needy, we are all helping ourselves to a smorgasbord of entitlements that we can't pay for and most could do without. Whether we like it or not, necessity will dictate that we sort out which is which. Instead of making those hard choices, we added the prescription drug benefit in 2003, stacking up another $8 trillion dollars of future debt. This plan, instead of using a needs-based sliding scale, gives everyone a benefit regardless of need, and was also widely seen as a gift to the pharmaceutical lobby. Passed by a Republican Congress and President, it proves that entitlement greed is bipartisan.

Many of faith have painfully witnessed those in power, especially conservatives, laying sole claim to the morals and values debate. The argument of separation of church and state notwithstanding, it is difficult to comprehend how it is left to the supposedly more secular "bleeding heart" liberals to aid the less fortunate when the word "poor" appears more than 500 times in the New Testament, more than almost any other word. Humility and service to others defined the life of Jesus. It should be the unquestioning duty of any self-professed "Christian" nation, or indeed of anyone of faith or conscience, to pass on to the less fortunate the gifts life bestows.

Those who decry the social "safety net" as socialism miss the point. The vast growth in the US economy has accrued almost entirely to the wealthy, even as worker productivity is the highest ever. The syndrome of working and middle class people having to work two or three jobs to make ends meet sharply contrasts with the families of just a generation ago who were able to live comfortably on one salary. Middle class quality of life has significantly eroded within our lifetime, while wealth at the top echelon has increased exponentially. From 2000 to 2006, 70% of income gains went to the top 1% of earners.

The "creative destruction" of capitalism is all about rewarding success and punishing failure. But what name do you give to a system where all our gains in worker productivity have enriched the wealthy at the expense of everyone else? The increasing numbers of the working poor

Chapter 5: Bubblenomics

are an indication that the social contract has broken down. This rise in poverty can be seen at every level and threatens to undermine the economy by eroding the stability of the workforce.

A good example is unemployment insurance, which only helps one out of every three workers who lose a job. American capitalism has always been good at re-inventing itself, but this is usually done by easily shedding redundant workers, something that cannot be done in Europe and Japan. It makes sense to compensate for this by providing workers better support during job transition. As real wages fall, more families are unable to meet their most basic needs. As well as being morally correct, it simply makes good business sense to have the economy work for people who do most of the work, not just for the wealthy elite.

The idea that the economic drain on the middle class is the result of too much coddling of the "undeserving lazy and poor" is pure propaganda. The reality is that the giant sucking sound from your piggy bank is the sound of your hard-earned money being sucked **up**, not down.

Throughout his campaign, Obama was saddled with the idea that he was out to "redistribute" wealth. Taxes are, by their nature, a redistribution of wealth, and any and all taxes are exactly that. The question remains, how is the redistribution to take place? Larry Summers, former Clinton Treasury Secretary (and current head of Obama's economic team), has calculated that the net effect of tax code from 1979 to today, and other economic factors, have resulted in the annual redistribution of $600 billion from the bottom 80% of earners to the top 1%. That $600 billion works out to about $8,000 per year for the average taxpayer. This same effect could be simulated by you and 50 or 60 of your closest friends taking $8,000 each, sealing the money in envelopes, and mailing them each year to someone who had a net income of $10 million or more.

Entitlements and Complacency

> *"I have absolutely no idea what my generation did to enrich our democracy. We dropped the ball. We entered a period of complacency and closed our eyes to the public corruption of our democracy."* — Wynton Marsalis

"Entitlement" is a complicated word. It engenders sharp opinions about who is owed what by whom. The dictionary definition of "entitlement" is "a government program that guarantees and provides benefits to a particular group," or "a right granted by law or contract." If one Googles the word "entitlement," most results highlight pieces complaining about poor people who feel "entitled to be rescued" by the more well-to-do; or about the so called "entitlement generation."   Fixing our broken economic order starts with sorting out exactly how we got here, and where the lines of responsibility lie.

Chapter 5: Bubblenomics

Although the "entitlement generation" is defined by demographers by birth year, it's bigger than that. Entitlement mentality is an inter-generational dysfunction, and is not difficult to spot. Case in point: the Iraq war. If justifications for fighting the war in the first place are completely put aside (difficult, I know), what makes it OK to cut taxes and then borrow the money to fight a war? Is it right to fight a war with an all-volunteer (poor and working class people) army so small that soldiers have to rotate through combat duty three or four times? We honor our servicemen and women and greatly appreciate their service, but where is the sense of shared sacrifice? If the Bush administration had raised taxes to properly fund the war, and instituted a draft to raise an army large enough to properly fight and win it, the entitled generation would never have re-elected him. In fact the war that "someone else" should pay for and "someone else" should fight, would never have happened.

Our crumbling infrastructure of roads and bridges were built and paid for (imagine that!) by hardworking Americans of the 50s. They raised families in silly little 1,300 sq. foot bungalows, but managed to build the interstate system which we, living in our McMansions, cannot even afford to maintain. Talk of patriotism and love of country falls easily from our lips, but can we stop having fun long enough to ensure the strength of our own survival?

The energy crisis is not one of energy. It is a crisis of complacency. After our wake-up call during the 70s oil embargo, how could we have spent the last 30 years asleep at the switch? We're now in a position where we'll have to pay oil-rich countries something like $10 trillion dollars over the next 15 years for oil. This represents the largest transfer of wealth in history from the United States to countries that are neither democracies nor friendly to the US. What kind of numbness would cause people to chant "drill baby drill," when they finally "get" the realities of oil supplies? Our answer is to deprive future generations of the last supplies of domestic oil, instead of using the time and money to develop alternative fuels? In the ten years it takes for these supplies to come online we had better already have an alternative energy plan in place. Someone will lead the way into that future, and right now it doesn't look like it's the United States. That unpleasant fact of life, right up there with our debt, is a critical national security concern.

Our new homes are not much more efficient than they were 50 years ago, even though super-insulated houses that use low-tech approaches to reduce energy consumption, by as much as 80%, have been common in Canada and Europe for 30 years. Canada's R-2000 home building program is an excellent example of how intelligent government regulations yield positive innovations in the marketplace. This program gives builders a cash incentive to build an energy-efficient house that meets very rigorous test standards (a much higher standard than "Energy Star"). The result has been

Chapter 5: Bubblenomics

"ground up" innovation; the builders themselves have competed with one another to bring this high standard to the consumer for the least amount of money. The R-2000 homes sell for about 10-20% more than regular homes and use 70% less energy. Over 20 years, more than 10,000 such homes have been built.

A widely-implemented domestic energy program would have multiple benefits. It would improve national security by reducing dependency on foreign oil. Tens of thousands of working class jobs would be created. And, aside from the obvious energy savings for the consumer, it creates competition for energy providers. Reducing the need for energy makes multiple options available. This would allow us to cut our umbilical cord to "big energy" of any kind, foreign or domestic.

Unfortunately, so far, the US has either done nothing about introducing a high standard of energy efficiency into building standards, or acted in ways that are detrimental. A recent building code change requiring an advanced level of hurricane protection on new houses was recently implemented from Florida to Maine. While such a level of protection is surely needed from the Chesapeake to Florida, the implementation of this new code further north, where large hurricanes are far less common, speaks volumes about how Washington lobbyists get what they want. Most of the damage from hurricanes in the northeastern US coast are caused by water, not wind, and is limited almost completely to waterfront homes and marinas. The oceanfront town I live in is full of houses hundreds of years old, and no one I know has ever seen or heard of a house being destroyed or even significantly damaged by wind alone.

This new standard adds tens of thousands of dollars to construction costs for no purpose that reason or statistics will bear out. The insurance lobby practiced what amounts to legalized extortion by the wholesale cancellation of home insurance in these areas, forcing homeowners into state-administered insurance pools at 2-3 times the rates they were paying. The new building code was then forced through on a state-by-state basis in a climate of fear.

Although the actual dollar effect on the price of new homes is still unclear, some estimate it could be as much as $40,000. Putting that same amount of money toward higher energy standards would have the far more important effect of saving energy for the entire history of that house's life, and for generations to come.

Energy-reducing technology has been available for decades. It is inexpensive, much of it is low-tech, and it would create hundreds of thousands of new jobs if widely implemented. New energy codes now coming into force across the country are pathetically out of date, and will not dramatically effect our energy dependence. There is no lobby for energy efficiency because it represents the decentralization of energy needs.

This is where government policy needs to rise to the greater common good instead of adding needless layers of bureaucracy, like this new hurricane code, at the behest of corporate lobbyists. In the 1960s and onward, computer chip costs were reduced from ten dollars to ten cents largely by government and military intervention. The computer revolution might never have taken place on its own. Similar types of government intervention could kick-start solar, wind, and energy-efficient buildings and appliances, which are already starting to become feasible purely in economic considerations.

— Chapter Six —

Hoodwinked and Hijacked

> "Like any debtor who borrows more year after year with no plausible way to reverse the trend, a nation sinking deeper and deeper into debt enters into an adverse power relationship with its creditors: greater and greater dependency." — William Greider

The Teetering Balance of Trade

A particularly troubling aspect of our current indebtedness is the amount of it financed by foreign countries, mostly China and Saudi Arabia. The difference between what we sell to other countries and what we buy from them is expressed as the Balance of Trade, which has been in deficit every year since 1971. We are buying more than we are selling. It went as high as $151 billion in 1987 but then ranged from $30–$90 billion during the Clinton years. Since then it has risen dramatically, and it now approaches $800 billion. Someday, our trading partners are going to own a lot of our wealth, especially when we are not saving any money and the government must borrow money every year to pay the bills. We are essentially borrowing money from the Chinese to buy their goods. Guess who China's sixth largest trading partner in the world is? That would be Walmart. Eventually we are going to "owe our soul to the company store."

Investor Warren Buffett is famously outspoken about the trade deficit. He uses the analogy of a rich family that owns a large farm, but consumes 4% more than they produce (about where we stand now). Each year they must sell a chunk of the farm and increase the mortgage on what they still own so they can pay for what they consume. At first it seems trivial, but eventually they lose majority control of the farm to their debtors. This cautionary tale is already happening. The world now owns a staggering $2.3 trillion more of us than we own of them. To look at the $700 billion dollar trade deficit another way, America is losing its wealth at the rate of almost $2 billion a day. At the end of World War II, almost all our debt was held by Americans. In 2007, foreigners owned almost 45% of our debt. If they decide America is becoming a credit risk, they could raise the interest on the debt, making our foreign debt even worse. The opposite could happen if the dollar keeps dropping: Our debt, which they own, becomes worth far less to them, which would greatly destabilize our relationship with China.

Chapter 6: Hoodwinked and Hijacked

Robbing the Common Man

> "The two greatest obstacles to democracy in the United States are, first, the widespread delusion among the poor that we have a democracy, and second, the chronic terror among the rich, lest we get it."
> — Edward Dowling, 1941

Fiscal conservatism used to be the heart and soul of the Republican Party. But that implies cutting both taxes and government services, preventing government from becoming a bloated entitlement machine that sucks the vigor out of free enterprise. The propensity of Democrats to add entitlements used to be offset by that fiscal conservatism. Today's Republican Party wants tax cuts but will not relinquish entitlements. Underlying that is a disturbing indication of personal greed: "I want less money taken from me by the government but I still want my entitlements and I don't care who else pays for them."

A politically brilliant ploy of the Republican Party has been to co-opt the working and middle classes being robbed of their wealth into voting for the robbers. Using "hot button" issues like gay marriage, gun rights and small-town values, Republicans have convinced "middle America" that their way of life was under attack from welfare cheats, mushy-brained liberals, media, and Hollywood elites. Whoever. Fill in the blanks. The Republican Party is the last line of defense! Even the religious right was co-opted. What did Republicans ever really accomplish for them?

In private conversations, Bush administration officials, and especially Karl Rove, are reported to have repeatedly mocked the religious right. Every issue the religious right cared about was carefully danced out the door.

Meanwhile, supply-side economics has accomplished the largest redistribution of wealth in modern history, with the willing participation of at least the Republican half of those robbed. The "tax and spend" liberals have all this while presided over the only administration (Clinton's) in 30 years to present a quasi-balanced budget, reduce the trade deficit and reduce the national debt. Just don't expect "small government" from Democrats.

Democrats never got much respect for being the only administration in recent years to show some fiscal restraint. The 2008 election featured McCain and "Joe the plumber" repeatedly accusing Obama of wanting to redistribute the wealth, as if all the Republican tax cuts to the rich were somehow not redistribution. Seeing McCain embrace the same Bush tax cuts that he opposed in his 2000 presidential run is just another example of how politicians' values end up in the Party meat-grinder.

On the flip side, Democrats also refuse to talk seriously about reducing government spending because, after all, their entire platform is all about expanding government. As detrimental as the Democrats' bad spending habits have been, they have not done as much damage as Republicans, who bankrupted us with tax cuts for the wealthy and failure to reign in their own spending.

Chapter 6: Hoodwinked and Hijacked

And give the Democrats some credit for ulterior motives tending towards the more altruistic.

As the Obama administration assumed power at the start of 2009, they admitted the stark reality of continued $1 trillion dollar deficits well into the future. That became clear as they unveiled the first of the bailout and stimulus plans. Republican Congressional leaders begrudgingly admitted the necessity of the spending, adding that these were debts that would be forced on the next generation. It has been a long time since any leaders have uttered this obvious truth. The inescapable next step, cutting spending, is only now being seriously discussed, and still only as something that has to be done sometime in the future. Cutting waste and earmark spending (which represented only $14 billion in 2008) would help, yet neither party has shown themselves capable of even that small first step. Why would they? Voters are angry about government spending but will not tolerate the loss of their own entitlements. Earmark spending is only a considered a waste of money in someone else's district. Some politicians defend earmark spending, saying it is the only way they can directly influence the budgetary process and bring jobs and money home to their districts.

This unsustainable public debt makes the US utterly dependent on countries like China and Saudi Arabia, who, at least for now, are still willing to carry the debt. You talk about your foreign policy crisis! No one wants to admit the amount of across-the-board sacrifice that will be necessary to put our house back in order.

Trickle-down: The Failure of Supply-side Economics

> "Madness is rare in individuals - but in groups, political parties, nations, and eras it's the rule." — Freidrich Nietzsche

"Trickle-down," also known as "supply-side economics," was first widely introduced into the political forum by Ronald Reagan. The central concept is that cutting taxes will stimulate so much economic growth that tax receipts will actually rise. It's worth noting that the supply-side theory did not come out of some lofty conservative think tank. Paul Krugman, in his book, *Peddling Prosperity*, says that "supply-side" was hatched during a series of dinner parties at a Manhattan restaurant. Most of its early adopters were self-appointed economists. As such, they neither argued before scientific conferences nor submitted papers for peer review, and no American universities contained any departments or professors devoted to supply-side theory. They still don't. The mainstream of academia, including most conservative economists, has long regarded supply-side as a crank theory. In fact, it's not even a theory. Theories have to be proven in a scientifically rigorous manner. Supply-side has never withstood this level of scrutiny; it is nothing more than conjecture. But, in spite of never having any respect outside of a small core of Republican ideologues, supply-side profoundly altered the political and economic landscape of America.

Chapter 6: Hoodwinked and Hijacked

Traditional conservative theory always favors reducing taxes, but only when matched by offsetting spending cuts. This was the "starve the beast" hypothesis, the idea that reduced revenues will force government to downsize. Supply-siders, on the other hand, posited that deficits were not important. The resulting economic gains would grow past the deficit. Supply-side has remained in the political mainstream even though it has never worked, because it contained a popular political message: you can cut taxes without any corresponding spending sacrifice. Yes, and you can lose weight without diet or exercise, too!

David Stockman, Reagan's budget director, was the person most responsible at first for selling supply-side to the public. Stockman was a "wunderkind," a boy genius. He came at Congress with a blizzard of statistics explaining how it would all work. Everyone was mesmerized, except the wizard himself. Stockman was the first to doubt as the revenue boost failed to happen. As early as December 1981, in an *Atlantic Monthly* article, Stockman admitted that "tax cuts were always a Trojan horse to bring down the top rate for the wealthy." By 1986, in his book, *The Triumph of Politics: Why the Reagan Revolution Failed*, Stockman boasted "It was all a performance."

One of the few supply-siders with a degree in economics was Art Laffer. He was one of the principle architects of the theory, and the inventor of the "Laffer Curve," which purported to prove how tax cuts would grow revenues. Over the course of many years and several administrations, the curve has never worked. Revenues grow, but only at a third of the rate that the deficit grows. Supply-siders love to pull up a graph that shows revenues increasing over the Reagan years. "Dynamic scoring," which factors in all other variables, takes the same graph and extracts revenue increases resulting from inflation and population growth. No year, or period of years, featuring supply-side tactics comes close to paying for the tax cuts. Supply-side in practice becomes nothing more than a tax holiday for the wealthy that someone else will have to fund. Laffer still does the rounds of the financial talk shows and still clings to his long-disproved theory, although recently he has changed his tune. He now claims that Reagan and Bush had practiced an extreme form of supply-side that he was never in favor of.

All evidence to the contrary, every Republican president has still claimed supply-side works. In September 2007, George W. Bush told Fox News that his tax cuts had "yielded more tax revenues, which allows us to shrink the deficit." The official Republican Party platform still lists in its top 10 talking points: "Reductions in top marginal tax rates [that] lead to greater revenues in the long run." Never mind ideological arguments. This position contradicts the cold hard facts over long periods of time. Yet in the Republican Party, dissent from this view is not tolerated. The Bush II administration was famous for accepting only preconceived answers that fit the Republican Party ideology. That tax rates affect people's behavior is not the part of supply-side that fails. The failure lies in taking a "reasonable" idea to

Chapter 6: Hoodwinked and Hijacked

unreasonable lengths. Spending discipline doesn't even have a seat at this table. By the twisted logic of supply-side, if government spending gets out of control, just cut more taxes to pay for it.

Oddly enough, Reagan started as a serious deficit hawk. He began his term by lamenting the deficit he had inherited ($1 trillion) and searched for a way to convey a trillion dollars to the American people. "A few weeks ago I called such a figure, a trillion dollars, incomprehensible, and I've been trying ever since to think of a way to illustrate how big a trillion really is. And the best I could come up with is that if you had a stack of thousand-dollar bills in your hand only four inches high, you'd be a millionaire. A trillion dollars would be a stack of thousand-dollar bills 67 miles high." How he ended up surrounded by kooks who convinced him to abandon deficit discipline, who knows? By the end of his first term, the deficit had doubled to $2 trillion. The debt of 39 previous presidents had been doubled in four years. But in supply-side ideology, deficits were not to be worried about. By the end of Reagan's second term a third trillion was added, and George H. W. Bush added a fourth. (Clinton began to pay down the debt for the first time in a generation.) When George W left office, he had taken his father's deficit and Reagan's deficit, plus the debt of 3 9 previous presidents, and **doubled** all of that again.

The only time government spending has been taken seriously was with "PAYGO," the policy of adding new programs only if they were paid for by new taxes.

This system of shared sacrifice was originally passed by the Democratic Congress in 1990 in the waning years of the first Bush presidency. Clinton then extended these budget enforcement restrictions in 1993 without a single Republican vote in favor. When budget surpluses first started to occur in 1998, Clinton attempted to prevent spending the portion of money allocated to Social Security with a "Save Social Security First" message. And who can forget Al Gore's famous "lockbox" in the 2000 Presidential Election? The lockbox was to contain the Social Security money, which would be taken out of the surplus and saved. And people laughed at Gore for this and elected George W. Bush instead. The bipartisan support for PAYGO was abandoned by Bush in 2001. The lockbox has never been spoken of again.

Jonathan Chait's 2007 book, *The Big Con: the True Story of How Washington got Hoodwinked and Hijacked by Crackpot Economics,* outlines how "the party of fiscal responsibility was transformed into the party of class warfare... A small cult of fanatical tax cutters... managed to get an iron grip on the ideological machinery of the conservative movement."

The "trickle-down" aspect of supply-side argues that the wealthy will be best at taking extra cash and turning it loose on the economy, but there is no guarantee it will actually work this way. They may buy expensive foreign imports, invest in the Asian stock market, or simply put it in the bank. "Demand-side" economics, on the other hand,

Chapter 6: Hoodwinked and Hijacked

suggests that if taxes are cut, they should be cut for the lowest earners. Low-income workers spend virtually all of their income, ensuring almost 100% of the cut goes back into the economy. They buy products and services from companies owned by the wealthy, thereby creating a "percolate up" effect.

The supply-side argument, however weak on the face of it, perversely benefits the arguers. Bush's $1.6 trillion in tax cuts went mostly to the top 1% of earners, the very rich who loan money to the government to fund its debts. The resulting deficit (from removing money from the tax rolls without offsetting spending cuts) increases the demand for money borrowed to fund the resulting deficit and drives up the interest rates of all borrowing. This results in higher rates of return for those who own the money supply.

The bailout is just additional proof that trickle-down is still in firm control. The bailout is corporate welfare hiding behind free-market ideology. Give billions to Wall Street, to the people who caused the problem, and some of it will trickle-down to the common man. Profits are privatized and losses are socialized.

All the President's Men

> "Everything is changing. People are taking the comedians seriously and the politicians as a joke." — Will Rogers

The notion that those with immense financial power can survive a sea change in political leadership, and re-surface, was proven true with the nomination of Larry Summers to head Obama's National Economic Council. Summers is perhaps best known for several well-publicized comments. While representing the World Bank he implied that "Africa is under-polluted." and most notably had to resign as Dean of Harvard University after he quipped that girls are genetically unfit for math and science. But it's not these verbal gaffes that disturb. His economic track record is little better than Greenspan's. Summers began as a protégé of Martin Feldstein, one of Reagan's supply-side gurus, and served on Reagan's Council of Economic Advisors. This puts him on the ground floor of this grand experiment of deregulation. Even though he has since been seen as a Democratic centrist, and has made some important comments on the dangers of wealth inequity, he has continued to lobby for deregulation.

In the early 90s Summers was stationed in Lithuania, newly liberated from the USSR. Summers was advising them on the transition to a market economy, a chance for him to test his economic theories on a grand scale. Less than two years later, Lithuania's economy was in shambles.

Chapter 6: Hoodwinked and Hijacked

They became the first and only former Soviet territory to freely vote their Communist oppressors back to power.

For his next act, Summers was at the World Bank with a team from Harvard, rescuing Russia's economy. The "rescue" concluded at the end of the 1990s with Russia having the largest debt default ever. On the Harvard team was Andrew Schleifer, his best friend and protégé from the Lithuania days. Schleifer misused his taxpayer-funded job to connect his hedge fund trader wife with billions in Russian profits. In 2000, the Justice Department sued Schleifer and Harvard for $102 million for conflict of interest. Summers used his connections to settle the suit for much less, getting his guy largely off the hook. (And, of course, later become the Dean of Harvard.) Another one of Summer's "Russia Dream Team" guys was Antoly Chubais, subsequently named the "most hated man in Russia." Chubais was in charge of Russia's privatization, and did it by selling State enterprises to insiders for a fraction of their worth, in blatantly rigged auctions. After the Russian market collapsed in 1998, Chubais was quoted by a Russian newspaper as saying: "we swindled them."

These financial misadventures drove Russian politics back into the hands of authoritarian oligarchs like Putin. Russia had had quite enough of Western Democracy. These Eastern Bloc meltdowns might have happened without Summer's involvement. But, considering the deregulatory blood on his hands, it's difficult to find a major policy initiative Summers has touched that has not ended in disaster. Summers financial disclosure reveals he earned over $5 million last year alone working for hedge fund trader D. E. Shaw, and made hundreds of thousands in speaking fees from J. P. Morgan Chase, Citigroup, Goldman Sachs, and Lehman Bros. over the years after his Harvard presidency. The pessimistic view is business as usual.

The new "go-to" guy at financial ground zero is new Secretary of the Treasury, Timothy Geithner. He is highly regarded as a bright, articulate, out-of-the-box thinker. But, as former chairman of the New York Fed, he's as tainted as anyone else who remained silent as Wall Street self-destructed. The SEC directly oversees the banks and brokerage houses, but the New York Fed is expected to raise red flags. That never happened. Geithner is seen as a bailout expert and was the architect of the AIG bailout, and engineered the sale of Bear Sterns. Neither of these transactions helped anyone but the ivory tower kings of finance, with taxpayers once again footing the bill. As a Summers/Rubin protégé and lifelong bureaucrat, he did his part to perpetuate the bubble. How is it that Geithner now deserves a promotion?

Why not promote Sheila Bair? The FDIC chairwoman was one of the first government officials in a key role to recognize the danger of subprime, urging immediate action as early as October 2007. When Indy Mac failed in July 2008, she temporarily halted all foreclosures on bank-

Chapter 6: Hoodwinked and Hijacked

owned mortgages, and has consistently advocated fixing the crisis by helping mortgagees first, before bankers and investors. She raised the cap on FDIC-insured deposits to $250,000 to save depositors' money from liquidation, and engineered the rescues of Washington Mutual, Wachovia and Indy Mac without any cost to the taxpayers or any loss of depositors' money. Bair did more during the early days of the crisis than any other single person in a position of power, and did so quickly, taking positive steps that helped everyone, not just wealthy traders.

Bair is not afraid to openly criticize the bailout, saying "We're attacking it at the [financial] institution level as opposed to the borrower level, and it's the borrowers defaulting. That is what's causing the distress at the institution level," she said. "So why not tackle the borrower problem?"

On Friday, November 14, 2008, Bair released details of her much more ambitious plan: a $24.4 billion program aimed at preventing 1.5 million foreclosures — even though Treasury Secretary Henry M. Paulson told reporters earlier in the week he would not fund it. Wall Street went ballistic over her mortgage rescue plan. A lifelong Republican with deep GOP Kansas roots, her work was praised by Democrats, but icily received by her fellow Republicans. Her term extends until 2013 and she is not required to step down for the new administration. Although a dark horse candidate for the Treasury Secretary job, she was ultimately not chosen, but hopefully we will see more of her work in the years to come.

Bair's attitude is that bankers and regulators must win back the public's trust because ultimately, public trust and consumer confidence are the economy's life support. In other words, it can't just be good for Wall Street; it has to be good for the public, or consumers won't buy it. If they don't, there is no recovery. As a pragmatist, she realizes that bailing out homeowners might also involve bailing out some undeserving mortgage-holders. But doing so will put more money back into the base of the economy than any big bank bailout. Besides that, it reaches the heart of what's causing the failure. The more mortgages that don't fail, the more mortgage securities don't fail. As the only consumer-focused person involved in the bailout, Bair's public and professional reputation is the only one among the key players that is rising.

Meanwhile, the "lone voice in the wilderness," Brooksley Born, calling for derivatives reform more than ten years ago has been vindicated. Recently asked what that felt like, she said "I am very sorry that it turned out I was right, because it has been a disaster for a lot of people who have lost a lot of money. I think there are still other disasters like that waiting to happen until Congress reforms the law and allows some federal oversight of this market." Born would have been another good candidate for Treasury. Some have suggested that being passed over for Attorney General in Clinton's day gave her the fire of her convictions at her Commodity Futures and Trading Commission (CFTC) job, which previously had been a relatively toothless agency. But she retired six years ago, and while active in women's law issues, it's unlikely she would accept such a major public service role.

Seeing so many "Clintonista" appointees in the new administration has not inspired confidence in Obama's change agenda. This change was to be a sweeping reform, not just a change of underwear. I'd like to believe that Obama plans to use these seasoned insiders to push a reform agenda, rather than using outsiders who might take a year or two to get up to speed. If this is true, there needs to be some sort of *mea culpa* by the old guard, as a signal for those who trusted the change message that something will, indeed, change. There has been precious little "ownership" for what went on. However, to move forward, we need to forgive or at least forget. But we can't forget without believing the perpetrators of this disaster realize what they have done, and want to make amends. The first person brave enough to fall on their sword will be the first person to be forgiven by the public.

So far, here in April 2009, the bailout looks like Bush II and the Stimulus looks like trying to spend our way out of a spending problem.

— Chapter Seven —

Where Do We Go from Here?

> "The Democrats seem to be basically nicer people, but they have demonstrated time and again that they have the management skills of celery. They're the kind of people who'd stop to help you change a flat, but would somehow manage to set your car on fire. I would be reluctant to entrust them with a Cuisinart, let alone the economy. The Republicans, on the other hand, would know how to fix your tire, but they wouldn't bother to stop because they'd want to be on time for Ugly Pants Night at the country club." — Dave Barry

The Good Life Is Hard Work

The road back depends on where we plan to return. The last two runs of prosperity, the dot-com boom and the housing boom, were both based on financial illusions. You would think, by now, we would have had enough of that. Apparently not. Long-entrenched ways of thinking are not that easily undone. We're still looking for the easiest possible fix. After three decades of prosperity financed by deficits, we are waking up to the reality of having no margin for error. Our answer? Democrats want to borrow and spend. Republicans want to cut taxes. Both approaches reveal hide-bound thinking that cuts straight along traditional party lines. Both parties still show a disturbing stubbornness. They're more interested in directing the stimulus toward their own agendas rather than do what's best to help the country.

Democrats appeared overly-eager to fund pet programs that have been starved under ten years of Republican leadership. Too many parts of the stimulus seemed an opportunistic attempt to push their social engineering agenda. Some of this spending is needed, as parts of society are hurting. But none of it has ever been "means-tested." Evaluating social programs for their effectiveness versus their cost, not to mention "can we afford to pay for it," is not part of the agenda.

The cursory attempt at reaching across the aisle was feeble at best. Democrats were clearly enjoying "sticking it to" the GOP. But, that's not something the American people are interested in seeing; if anything it causes us to lose confidence that anything good can ever come of the legislative process. The Democrats did make a good case for "structural" spending that will help rebuild our crumbling infrastructure, something no generation, especially a prosperous one, has the right to ignore. Other spending, such as propping up the social safety net, is the duty of any civilized society faced with a citizenry fallen on hard times not necessarily of their own making. And, especially when rising wealth inequity is increasingly turning us into a nation of haves and have-nots. After all, if wealthy investors are getting their bailouts, the average person on the street could expect some help as well.

Republicans kept calling for tax cuts, no surprise there. For the first time in 30 years though, some of the cuts they called for were for the little guy, like cutting payroll taxes.

Chapter 7: Where Do We Go from Here?

Even though 40% of the stimulus was tax cuts, and Obama took heat from his own party for it, Republicans were still not satisfied. They showed the American people how far they are from abandoning the failed trickle-down ideology. Many top Republicans are finally admitting that their party has strayed from its traditional roots of limited government, fiscal discipline, and personal responsibility. But they have no recent history of cutting or eliminating government programs (except for family planning) to offset tax cuts, and they still aren't suggesting that now. Tax cuts are, of course, no help to the unemployed.

The familiar and worn-out phraseology coming from people like House Minority Leader John Boehner, was that Obama tax increases to the wealthy would throttle the recovery. "People earning over $250,000 already pay over 60% of the taxes." Missing from his comment is that they make 80% of the money. The average Wall Street tycoon pays a lower income tax rate than a waitress, because the tax rate for dividends and investments is so low.

A big deal was made during the election about how Obama's plan to raise taxes for those with income over $250,000 would hurt small businesses. In reality, only 8.9% of small businesses make over $250,000. Even when Bush's rollback of the top two tax rates expires in 2010, very few small business owners will see their rates go up, because only 1.9% of them fall into these top two tax tiers.

If tax relief for the wealthy created jobs, surely that would have been seen in the last eight years. Yes, unemployment was low. But most of those "trickle-down" jobs are minimum wage. Families needed two full-time workers to live even a modest lifestyle. Cutting taxes for the wealthy did nothing but drain the treasury and stagnate all other social classes. Once Republicans run out of "hot button" social issues to rally middle America, they might realize just how far they have strayed from their conservative roots.

In his acceptance speech, Obama chastised America for a "collective failure to make the hard choices." That single phrase nails it. Two generations removed from the "greatest generation," we are the weakest generation. We refuse to admit the good life is not a birthright. To quote "Motley Fool": "The line-ups at Starbucks are still annoyingly long. The music has stopped but the party's still kicking."

Even in the best of times, the good life is hard work. When times get tough, the work gets harder, the sacrifices greater. There has been nothing in the stimulus package, in the bailouts, nor in any of the debate surrounding the economic collapse that reflects this simple reality.

Chapter 7: Where Do We Go from Here?

Stop Doing Everything You've Been Doing

> A Native American grandfather talking to his young grandson tells the boy he has two wolves inside of him struggling with each other. The first is the wolf of peace, love and kindness. The other wolf is fear, greed and hatred. "Which wolf will win, grandfather?" asks the young boy. "Whichever one I feed," is the reply." — Native American proverb

The old joke goes, "If you break your leg in three places, you better stay away from those places." Silly, but probably the best advice for returning to some semblance of stability and sanity. The lesson is to stop doing almost everything we've been doing.

Time was, credit, any credit, was bought dearly. In the 50s, you needed to sign away your firstborn to buy a TV set on credit. Government debt was carefully controlled because our money was tied to the gold standard. When we fought World War II we darn well had to pay for it. But things changed. First there were layaway and installment plans, then there were credit cards, then there were loans with "no money down," and so on. Those with the means to make their money work for them convinced (conned) us that we could finance prosperity on credit. And just as any con man will tell you, you can't con someone unless they have a little greed in themselves, too. So we bought the credit.

But gold is a harsh master. The gold standard did not allow the government to print money at will. Gold makes you do everything the hard way. We didn't want the hard way. Ever since prehistoric man crawled from caves, it's been all about making things easier. So, we ditched the gold standard in 1971, and ushered in the Era of Entitlement.

Sure, we had our ups and downs, but our new easy money system meant the expansion of our money supply (and lifestyle) was now as inevitable as it was unstoppable. After all, if you could create money from nothing, why wouldn't you?

The world noticed what a good time we were having in our cozy little entitlement era, and soon everyone was "Jonesing" for a piece of the action. Our massive credit run-up could not have occurred without most of the world worshiping the greenback. The strength of the American economy, not the metal it used to be tied to, was the new "gold standard." Goodwill was now the only thing behind the greenback. So revered was that goodwill, the World happily financed our spending spree.

Precarious financial models were built upon the idea that the upward spiral would continue indefinitely. An upward spiral bought on credit and easy money. There were credit default swaps, deficit spending, and "no money down" mortgages. Can't qualify for one mortgage? Get two smaller ones and buy that house you can't afford. Take advantage of zero percent introductory rates, airline mile rewards for spending, and easy tear-off checks in credit card

Chapter 7: Where Do We Go from Here?

statements encouraging instant cash advances. It became a high-stakes economic slot machine. Rooms full of green eyeshades, shirt-sleeved accountants were replaced with hopped-up money junkies inventing ways to spin the economy fast enough to blur reality. Then we got sick.

Good times often end in hangovers, and ours is worth trillions. $2.5 trillion. After our three-decade spending spree, that's how much more the World owns of us than we own of them. We need to enter a 12-step program for credit abusers. But we're not alone. The world has a hangover too. The world is not sure what happened last night, but whatever it was, it wasn't good. The world will no longer be sweet-talked by the likes of us.

Well, we're feeling a little violated too. We are staggering around in a numbed stupor, throwing billions around as if we had billions. Turns out, all this deficit spending means the Fed has to print even more money. Never mind the $700 billion bailout that Congress keeps changing, the Fed has shored up banks with loans and guarantees that some say now approaches $9 trillion. Even if it ever gets paid back, when the Fed creates that money from nothing, it hands the taxpayers the interest bill, and the privately-owned wealthy Fed becomes wildly more wealthy. According to the *Wall Street Journal*, the Fed's balance sheet total (which is all we see of the inner workings) showed $905.7 billion of assets as of Labor Day 2008, and as of December 20, 2008 showed $2.31 trillion. But, according to the *Wall Street Journal*, much of that is collateral from

-143-

bailouts, and that asset material is "mystery meat" acquired from the likes of Bear Stearns and AIG, so who knows what it's really worth? Live by the sword...

The massive infusions of bailout money to private banks are not kick-starting credit or anything else. The bailed-out banks, for the most part, have no obligation to say how they are using the money, or to even repay it. The obligation will be ours. We will endure years of economic hardship for a bank welfare program to fund their negligence. And we have a gnawing feeling the bailout's purpose is not to provide banks money so they can feed us mortals more credit (which we're trying to quit anyway). The more likely reality is that the bailout money is really meant to reimburse wealthy investors for lost equity.

Just how did so many Wall Street geniuses get it so wrong? In the words of Paul O'Neil, who even as Treasury Secretary was famously suspicious of the financial sector: "They were all kind of floating up there in the ether... It just felt really good, and they were making all this money... In truth, very few of them understood the business activity that was going on."

Much of the bailout money sent to AIG ended up passing right through AIG and going straight to banks like Goldman Sachs, Germany's Deutsche Bank, France's Société Générale, and others, for massive payouts owed to these banks under the "Credit Default Swap" insurance policies the banks had invested in. It is not clear whether the government had any idea billions of bailout money for AIG would go directly to these "counterparties," let alone to payees that were foreign banks.

Chapter 7: Where Do We Go from Here?

Problem one is the murky nature of the bailout payouts, given in secrecy with no checks or balances. Problem two is that the payouts went to pay these obligations to the banks at 100 cents on the dollar in what is essentially a bankruptcy situation, as AIG would be finished without these bailouts. Meanwhile, average private investors in the stock market have seen their invested savings cut in half due at least in part to the meltdown caused by companies like AIG.

What kind a bankruptcy is it when the bankrupt company gets money with no questions asked, and then pays out debtors in full? (In typical bankruptcies, creditors get a fraction of that.) If it was your money, wouldn't you be a tougher negotiator? It is your money! This one case illustrates, perhaps better than any other, why the bailout is so faulty. The government has no idea what it's really doing when it tries to kick-start an area of the free market that no one understood in the first place. The bailout is being engineered, by the wealthy, to go straight to wealthy investors, while average people receive little or no help for financial calamities they had very little to do with.

There Are No Atheists in Foxholes

> *"The Market is a place set apart where men may deceive each other."*
> — Diogenes Laertius, 200 AD

The bailout is the epitome of entitlement behavior. It's called the "miracle of free markets" when they make oodles of money manipulating the economy in strange and wonderful ways. But when they screw up, and the stock market renders its judgment, they won't accept it. Just like the old saying "there are no atheists in foxholes," how easily free marketers become Socialists when their own butts are on the line.

Those of us inhabiting the real world are still trying to process why no one saw this crisis coming. Not the Fed, the Treasury, or anyone else in charge. Now they're asking us to take their word on bailing out a system they didn't really understand, based on some vague threat of global collapse. Seems like that's happened anyway. And don't bet that they will see the hyperinflation coming either; that is inevitable at the rate the Fed is manufacturing funny money.

Paul O'Neil again, on rating the Obama bailout: ..."I think the administration hasn't gotten to the point yet of insisting that the big 19 financial institutions put their cards on the table. If I was buying a company... I would go and look in the boiler room and find out if there's rust on the valves. I think knowing how bad it is is the only way we're going to

Chapter 7: Where Do We Go from Here?

create a foundation for going forward... There's not enough ink in the printing presses of the Federal Reserve to print enough money to fill the void created by the absence of real economic growth."

Let the great national kitchen table debates begin. When the fruits of hard-working ordinary people can be plundered by wealthy elites, doesn't that make us peasants in a world of robber barons? A revolution of consciousness is in order. Just a few years ago, the "green" and "alternative energy" movements were thought by many to be a bunch of "kooks" at the fringes of society. In just a few short years, green and clean has entered the mainstream of thought and practice in a big way, and will only grow more prevalent. In the same way, if we demand fiscal sanity, and demand it long and hard enough, eventually we might get it.

Short Takes

> "It may well be that our means are fairly limited and our possibilities restricted when it comes to applying pressure on our government. But is this a reason to do nothing? Despair is not an answer. Neither is resignation. Resignation only leads to indifference, which is not merely a sin but a punishment." — Elie Wiesel

❏ **Failed companies should be allowed to fail.** Supervise the failure in an orderly manner, as was done in the savings and loan scandal, where the Resolution Trust Corp was set up to dismantle failing banks and dispose of their assets. The stock market has already rendered its judgment on these companies: they're dead. Seize the company, sort out the good parts from the bad parts; sell the good parts at auction and liquidate the bad. No exceptions. There is no good case for allowing companies that made such huge mistakes to survive. Trust and confidence will be almost impossible to resurrect until this happens, because allowing bad companies to fail is crucial to the survival of a free market system.

During Japan's liquidity crisis of the 90's, Alan Greenspan was advising them they had to let their banks fail in order to rebuild their economy. Instead, Japan propped up "zombie" banks and the Nikkei index is still languishing. Timothy Geithner claimed recently Japan's rescue didn't work because they didn't spend enough money on the problem. Japan did nothing but spend money bailing out failing companies, and it didn't work. It never has worked.

Chapter 7: Where Do We Go from Here?

No one gets it yet. The honorable thing to do is admit the mistakes, accept the bad medicine, and find the strength to rebuild from what is still good. The cowardly path is to prop up companies that have not earned the right to survive.

❑ **Efforts to re-inflate the bubble are a false promise.** This is the hard part. Our entire culture revolves around crass consumerism. We need to reassess the true value in our lives and just possibly learn to be happy without material excess. How crazy that the stimulus plan is being evaluated by how its individual parts will spur consumer spending ("good") and not savings ("bad"). Hello, aren't we close to being a bankrupt nation? Aren't many of us individually maxed out? Didn't our retirement savings just get cut in half? Is spending more money on foolish pleasures the best we can do to rebuild an economy that has lasting value? Maybe we need to dial this whole mess back to the 50s and start over. Maybe that will happen anyway!

❑ **Excessive corporate greed must be stopped.** Recent editorial commentary in the *Wall Street Journal*: "Many bank officials were caught off-guard by the depth of public ire against Wall Street bonuses." Astounding, but true. Even after all that's gone on, there was no awareness whatsoever among the top exectutives of bailed-out companies that taxpayers would be angry over the bonuses they awarded themselves!

The Age of Entitlement: How Greed and Arrogance Got Us Here

Most of these are public companies. As shareholders, we have the power to check corporate greed. Pull your money out of any company with excessive corporate pay. It makes sense anyway: When senior management gets rich no matter how the company performs, there will eventually be dysfunctionality at the top levels and the company will suffer. Speaking of dysfunctional: After the public shock over news reports of $18 billion in 2008 bonuses doled out to bailed-out companies, Rudy Giuliani suggested that skipping bonuses would mean a loss of jobs in Manhattan service industries. Words almost fail here. Why not just take the $18 billion and throw it out of car windows if you're worried about the commoners?

The continuing furor over executive bonuses at one company after the other on the brink of collapse shows how far these executives are from "getting it." Oh, but the bonuses are a contractual obligation! When automakers and airlines are being bailed out, it is standard operating procedure to break union and pilot comtracts to reduce pay. If AIG had not been bailed out, they would have ceased to exist and there would have been no pay, bonus or otherwise.

Not to mention the absurdity of calling a bonus a contractual obligation. Some companies plan to circumvent the bonus furor by calling the bonuses "retention awards," as if these executives and traders who brought the free world to its knees are worth retaining, or are in danger of being recruited by another firm. Another argument is that the bonuses should at least go to the traders who were operating

Chapter 7: Where Do We Go from Here?

under directions and assumptions from senior executives. Airline pilots and auto workers never even had the chance to try that excuse when stripped of their pay.

For executives used to life as robber barons, this is all very painful. Still, remorse or contrition is hard to find. The executive compensation plan being discussed by some companies for the future involves avoiding bad publicity by doing away with performance bonuses altogether and tripling or quadrupling base pay.

At AIG, Joe Cassano, the head of the unit most responsible for AIG's meltdown, was being paid a consulting fee of a million dollars a month in 2008, even after huge losses were sending the company straight over a cliff. Performance and pay has never been more disconnected than this.

❏ **Bail out failing mortgages.** People who made bad mortgage decisions are at least no worse than tycoons who made bad corporate decisions. Twenty million more homeowners will soon have homes worth less than the balance of their mortgage. They will have to choose between making the payments or walking away. Even a 3% decline in defaults preserves $500 billion in homeowner equity, which could in turn re-inject $40-50 billion of consumer spending back into the starved economy, double what it would cost for the rescue. It's a no-brainer.

A good rescue plan from two investment managers, Thomas Patrick and Mac Taylor, would have targeted the 1.1 million mortgages which will reset in the next several years and will in turn cause another round of potential mortgage defaults. This would, in turn, endanger the securities they are bundled into. This plan used no taxpayer money; it required sacrifices by both bankers and mortgage-holders. It would have been a win/win for banks, mortgagees and taxpayers. The bank takes a hit but likely a far gentler hit than another tsunami of defaults. The Obama administration has finally unveiled a modest mortgage rescue plan that relies on government to solve the problem instead of forcing banks to compromise. Whereas the banks were bailed out within days and weeks, it took months to get even a modest plan out to mortgage-holders.

❏ **Enact ethical and strict mortgage lending requirements.** Everyone knew that subprime lending standards were crazy; no one did anything about it. Excerpt from *Market Watch* column by Robert Schroeder, May 2007: "Senate Banking Committee Chairman Christopher Dodd (D-CT), has urged the Federal Reserve to require all mortgage originators to evaluate a borrower's ability to repay a loan before making a mortgage loan." Duh....

❏ **Outlaw the rating services.** Was anyone on Wall Street paying attention here? Having Moody's and Standard and Poor's paid by the issuers of stock to rate the stocks? If the ratings are deemed essential, they must somehow be independent ratings, paid for by investors or the public.

Chapter 7: Where Do We Go from Here?

❑ **Regulate derivatives.** If the sellers of these Credit Default Swaps, insurance that the debts won't default, had to back them with enough capital to pay out a default, or even a reasonable fraction of it, these deals would probably cease to exist. That's because they would be too expensive to buy for the protection they provide. Derivatives no longer serve any worthwhile purpose. Even the most sophisticated players obviously don't understand these complex deals, and their consequences are potentially catastrophic. They represent too much danger to have any value. It's like keeping a nuclear weapon under your bed for safety.

❑ **Re-establish traditional capital requirements.** The idea that banks and investment houses are their own best judge of acceptable risk has proved to be unacceptable. Not for a publicly-traded company. As John Kenneth Galbraith said, "Speculation buys out the available intelligence." Enough said.

❑ **Reform the SEC.** The stock market has far too much influence on the SEC. Most top regulators at the SEC know that if they don't rattle anyone's cage during their tenure, they will go on to lucrative jobs on Wall Street. To restore its credibility for protecting investors, the SEC must have experienced, respected investigators and executives. And, perhaps the revolving door should spin the other way. Instead of regulators going on to Wall Street jobs, retiring Wall St. executives should populate the SEC, if for no other reason than to give back valuable service to the shareholders who made them rich. Whether that level of altruism can be still be found on Wall Street is another question for another day.

❑ **Bring back Glass-Steagall.** The Depression Era law which separated banks from investment houses may have been outdated but it was obviously a huge mistake to scrap it. Lawmakers and regulators must take a good hard look at how the two entities can interact without both self-destructing.

❑ **Big Banking is over.** The financial universe used to orbit around big banks like Citibank. No more. As it turns out, Citibank was, in the words of Gretchen Morgenson, "too big to manage, too unwieldy to succeed and too gigantic to sell to one buyer." It turns out they never integrated their vast empire of services, so they had all the additional expenses and none of the advantages. The synergies of size never happened. Now they need to break themselves apart to survive.

We must prevent banks from getting so large that their failure is catastrophic to the entire system. We should never again be subjected to this kind of extortion. That smaller banks would make large deals between corporations impossible is not an excuse for the existence of large banks. Banks have acted in consortium before to accomplish big deals, and they can do it again.

❑ **American financial dominance is at risk.** At this moment, America looks an awful lot like an aging dinosaur superpower, too far globally extended and too entrenched in greed and stupidity to long remain the financial beacon of the world. The American free market creed has

Chapter 7: Where Do We Go from Here?

self-destructed, and international companies will be seeking more stability than the US stock market can provide for quite some time. The global balance of power is shifting. How ironic and symbolic that at the moment we are crawling on our knees, Chinese astronauts are spacewalking. American business has always been good at re-inventing itself. Now would be a good time to begin that difficult work. Remember that China right now has more "honors" students than America has people. Our standing as the world's only superpower is by no means guaranteed.

❏ **American innovation is falling behind.** Europe is far ahead of us in alternative energy and green technologies. Countries like Germany and Portugal are putting massive amounts of money into clean energy R&D, threatening to leave the US behind in the global race to invent the green technologies of the future. There is nothing more vital to long-term prosperity and security than to be at the forefront of the green revolution. The green and clean boom has already begun, and unlike the internet and housing booms which were relatively short-lived, this is a global exploding market with no end in sight. The US needs to get back into the business of producing something of value.

❏ **The US stock market has myopia.** Publicly-traded companies cannot see beyond tomorrow's stock close or next month's fiscal quarter. No one is positioning companies for long-term success except for a few prominent venture capital firms. A case in point is the US auto industry's failure to embrace hybrid and smart car technology.

While GM struggles to bring the Chevy Volt to market, a group of high school kids from one of the roughest neighborhoods in Philadelphia have built a handful of smart cars that blow away anything Detroit has done. Called the "West Philly Hybrid X Team" and led by shop teacher Simon Hauger, the team has created numerous award-winning hybrid vehicles. They won the "Tour del Sol" competition three times, beating out top universities and research institutes.

Last year's stunning success was the creation of a "hybrid supercar," built to disprove the misconception that all hybrid cars are turtles. Built on the chassis and body of the Slovakian "K1 Attack" roadster, and using a combination of a VW turbo diesel that runs on biodiesel and a 200 HP electric motor, the car gets 60 mpg, yet accelerates from 0-60 mph in under four seconds, making it faster than all but a few production cars in the world. The school"s automotive shop class modified the car using off-the-shelf parts for under $15,000. Their next project is a 100 mpg hybrid-biodiesel they are developing for the $10 million "Automotive X Prize."

If Hauger can find such talent in a crack-infested, inner-city neighborhood, why can't Detroit do it, and why can't the US stock market chase promising innovation like this instead of investing in useless financial trickery?

Chapter 7: Where Do We Go from Here?

❏ **Can morality be part of the market?** The failure of US financial markets was bigger than the failure of deregulation or laxity of mortgage lending standards. At its core was a massive collective failure of morality. There were entire rooms and buildings full of people who let greed override common sense and basic decency. And they did it repeatedly over a long period of time. For the long-term investor trying to build wealth, the feeling is that the stock market is a slot machine. As Jon Stewart says: "These guys were on a "Sherman's march" through their companies, financed by our 401Ks... they burned down the house and walked away rich as hell." By way of explanation, they claimed it was a once-in-a-lifetime tsunami that couldn't have been predicted.

It's no easier to explain a failure of this magnitude than it is to provide a solution, but acknowledgement of this failure by those involved would help. The fact that this has not yet happened reveals a stunning poverty of the soul by those in power.

❏ **Abolish the Fed.** The Federal Reserve manipulates the money supply which erodes Americans' standard of living, enlarges big government, and enriches well-connected elites. The United States Constitution grants to Congress authority to coin money and regulate the value of the currency. It does not give Congress the authority to delegate control over monetary policy to a privately-owned and controlled central bank. The existence of the Fed and its control over the lives of ordinary hard-working

Americans is exactly what our founding fathers **didn't** want. They had the courage to rebel against the tyranny of England and King George. We are now being colonized by the same kind of wealthy elites.

In 1914, Woodrow Wilson had this to say after the creation of the Fed and the enactment of income taxes: "I am a most unhappy man. I have unwittingly ruined my country. A great industrial nation is controlled by its system of credit. Our system of credit is concentrated. The growth of the nation, therefore, and all our activities are in the hands of a few men. We have come to be one of the worst ruled, one of the most completely controlled and dominated governments in the civilized world. No longer a government by free opinion, no longer a government by conviction and the vote of the majority, but a government by the opinion and duress of a small group of dominant men."

❏ **Bring back the Gold Standard.** Alan Greenspan said in 1967, "Deficit spending is simply a scheme for the confiscation of wealth. Gold stands in the way of this insidious process. It stands as a protector of property rights." How Greenspan got from defender of the gold standard to the loose money policy that has kept the printing presses rolling all these years is a mystery. With a gold standard we wouldn't need wizards like him, because gold money regulates itself. It would put a limit to government ability to spend, borrow, and create bloated government programs.

Chapter 7: Where Do We Go from Here?

Since money was uncoupled from the gold standard in 1971, the value of the dollar has inflated 300%, and the government has never balanced a budget. What is the effect of a dollar inflated 300%? Let's say Joe worked in a factory in 1971 at the age of 25 and made $17 an hour (a top-notch wage!). Today, almost ready for retirement, he still works in the same factory but now he makes $30 an hour. He is really only making $10 an hour in 1971 dollars. His real earning power is only 58% of what it was when he was 25.

As an illustration of the staying power of gold, consider this: Medieval texts have said that an ounce of gold could buy "a full suit of fine men's clothes." An ounce of gold today, at $900+, could still buy a good suit, shirt and tie, trench coat and shoes at a men's clothing store.

❏ **No more big spending programs.** Democrats: It doesn't make any sense to build "The Great Society" on our grandchildren's nickel. Republicans: Why didn't you veto a single spending bill when you had control of legislative and executive branches for six years and veto power over a Democrat-controlled Congress the next two years? Please, both parties, stop spending money we don't have. I have an idea: Rate every government program on a scale of one to ten, one being necessary for a civilized society and ten being "a perk." Then we can start adding them back in until we've spent our tax receipts and then... STOP! If we end up without a Department of Education, oh well. If we want it badly enough we'll have to to raise taxes to pay for it. Did we think we were so sophisticated that grade school accounting no longer applied to us?

❑ **No more tax cuts.** Borrowing money to cut taxes is so stupid as to numb the senses. Republicans spent their last 20 years in power doing just that, and now, when we really need a tax cut, we're too broke to have one. Let's get real here. Sen. Richard Burr, (R-NC) in the Republican response to President Obama's Feb 28th 2008 weekly radio address, accused Obama of "the single largest increase in federal spending in the history of the United States, while driving the deficit to levels that were once thought impossible."

It's difficult to know where to start a response to this. Most (by far) of the $10 trillion deficit was money spent under Republican control, most of it spent to give wealthy (Republicans) tax cuts. Most of this current deficit spending is to pull (Republican) fat-cats out of the fire. A relatively small portion of it will go to rebuild infrastructure that crumbled while the economy soared (for some), and to prop up the necessities of civilized life for the embattled average working person. For the average worker, income tax cuts are not as useful as you might think. Two-thirds of taxpayers pay more in payroll tax than income tax.

If I hear one more Republican complaining about how Obama's spending will have to be paid for by our children, I just might throw a nutty. Yes, it is true, but who did you think was paying for the last 17 tax cuts? While it is very difficult to get behind the level of spending coming out of our new Democratic White House, it's even harder to believe that Republicans have suddenly found fiscal responsibility.

Chapter 7: Where Do We Go from Here?

❏ **GOP and Dems must learn to get along.** Message to Congress: Your constituents voted for you, but as a whole the American people despise you. Democrats would be wise not to be as partisan as the Republicans have been, even if they can. This polarization is killing us. The public wants to believe that you will both "own" whatever solutions are put in place to try and dig us out. Then we might be able to act like we're all in this together. The behavior of Congress during the debate of the rescue and stimulus plans was just more of the same. Democrats did not try hard enough to include Republican ideas, but Republicans have to do a little better than trotting out the same old tax cuts. No more blaming; we're sick of it.

❏ **Reform Social Security and Medicare/Medicaid funding.** Just how much longer are we going to ignore this? Wisconsin Republican, Paul Ryan, put together a well-thought-out plan that adjusts Social Security benefits over time to keep the system solvent, and brings in a one-third personal investment element that has a guarantee not to be less than the benefit provided by the "in plan" Social Security benefit, and becomes the property of the retiree to either use or pass on. Ryan's overall plan, called "Roadmap for America's Future," is part of a comprehensive plan to reform taxes, control spending and put the brakes on runaway entitlement outlays.

John McCain had an excellent opportunity to embrace the plan in the summer of 2008. It would have given him some badly-needed credibility on the economy, and it would have introduced Ryan's ideas on the national stage. So far, repeated attempts to introduce this legislation have been ignored by both parties, even though Ryan was the ranking Republican on the Budget Committee. Now, with Democrats in charge, there is little likelihood this plan, the only serious recent proposal to deal with entitlements, will ever be discussed again.

❏ **Pay down the deficit.** How much is $1 trillion? If you started spending a million dollars a day on the day Jesus Christ was born, you would only be 75% done now. A credit counselor would tell us "start now, even just with small payments." We rode a wave of prosperity purchased on credit, and everyone owns a piece of that. Our politicians didn't talk about the deficit because we didn't. Now we need to incur even more debt for bailouts and stimulus packages, but we also need a plan to pay down the deficit. We need to make it very public. If we are all reminded of our public debt and are consciously paying it down, the public will finally "own" the debt, the way we did with war bonds in World War II. This needs to be a shared sacrifice. It's going to be painful, but maybe if it hurts real bad we won't do it again.

❏ **We're better off to assume they don't know anything.** May 2008, Fed Chairman Ben Bernanke: "...the effect of troubles in the subprime market will likely be limited to the central bank... [I don't] expect subprime market problems to spill over significantly into the rest of the economy or the financial system." These so-called experts that rise up through the system into positions of power may be very

Chapter 7: Where Do We Go from Here?

smart and talented. At what, I don't know. Don't necessarily bet though, that they have a better grasp on reality than you and I. Anyone in a position of power who claimed the economy was sound in the three months leading up to the meltdown should be ashamed of their ineptitude.

❑ **Restructure the bailout.** The excesses of this boom were predicated on the mass delusion that unlimited growth would continue as long as money kept getting pumped into the system. Never mind whether any real value was being created. Now, the next myth is that the orgy of money can be wound up again by throwing money at the same banks who squandered it. Recapitalizing banks that don't deserve it is bad enough; doing it by handing them the money in secret with no strings attached, and no limit to the extent, is indefensibly stupid. It would be easier for taxpayers to swallow if some of the bailout reached the little guy. We're all pretty weary by now of "trickle-down."

The other troubling aspect of the bank recapitalization is that some of the 22 banks who got the money are now swallowing smaller banks left to fend for themselves, and getting them for fire-sale prices. The bailed-out banks become the government's favored few and competition in the banking sector is reduced. A handful of big investors get bailed out and America's economic future gets concentrated into ever-fewer hands, and ever-bigger banks. Exactly the opposite of what might bring long-term stability to the economy.

Bailout II differs from Bailout I only in that it is less secretive. It stretches credulity to think Treasury Secretary Geithner, who authored the AIG bailout as Chairman of the New York Fed, was later surprised by the bonuses. If it truly was a surprise, it reveals why the government has no business taking over huge corporations; they have no idea how to manage the situation.

A bailout is only worthwhile if there is some hope the bailed-out company has a chance of survival on its own, and can then pay back the bailout. As James Grant, of Grant's Interest, says: "Capitalism without financial failure is not capitalism at all, but a kind of socialism for the rich."

❑ **Republican ideologues should stand down.** Blowhards like Republican pundits Grover Norquist and Rush Limbaugh are trying to hang Republican-created deficits around Obama's neck, and using words like "the Obama recession." Republicans: don't overestimate the gullibility of the public. Rebuild respect from the ground up by admitting how 20 years of Republican supply-side economics have bankrupted the treasury. Go back to being conservative deficit hawks. Without the deficit hawks there was no counterpoint to big-spending Democrats, and we went straight to deficit hell.

❑ **Income inequality will stall the recovery.** Excerpt from Obama's inauguration speech: "A nation cannot long prosper when it only favors the prosperous." Last year, 23% of national income went to the top 1% of earners. The last time inequality was so great was in 1929, just before the

Chapter 7: Where Do We Go from Here?

Great Depression. Stagnation of the working poor and the middle class starves the economic engine of the fuel it needs. A robust recovery will not happen until the working class and middle class feel comfortable again.

❏ **Banks must own their toxins.** Any stock recovery that does not revalue assets is a farce. No one will believe, especially now, in falsely-stated asset values. Without belief there is no trust, and, without trust there is no trade. "Mark-to-market" means that companies whose assets are invested must realistically state on today's balance sheet what these assets are worth in today's market. It's clear just how out-to-lunch banks are when they push to be exonerated from regulations that require them to "mark their assets to market." The scary thing is, some of these banks will be revealed to be insolvent even with the bailout. If we have to peel this thing back to trading with sea shells, then maybe that's where the build-back will have to start.

On April 2nd, as this book goes to press, The Federal Accounting Standards Board has loosened the mark-to market accounting standards. Now banks will be able to value their toxic assets at what they think they might fetch in a few years instead of what the market says they're worth now. The argument for altering the standard is that rapid devaluation of these assets exacerbated the financial decline, and led to banks balancing precariously on the edge of insolvency. In reality, greed and stupidity caused the devaluation of these assets, and to imagine that a less transparent accounting standard will cure that, is to believe in the tooth fairy.

❑ **Whose plan is "sketchy"?** Geithner's recovery plan was greeted by Wall Street with a 400 point plunge because the plan "lacked specifics." This, by a bunch whose plan was specifically to line their pockets with cash as they bailed out of their sinking ships. Let me get this straight. The Wall Street geniuses who drove the economy into the ditch now think they have the credibility to attack the plan to pull the bus out of the ditch? The irony and farce beggars description. Perhaps the previous Paulson bailout was more to their liking: "Throw money into our sinkhole and we'll tell you when to stop."

Why would the opinions of people who touted the robust economy be of any value whatsoever? Problem is, that will leave us being advised by Chauncey Gardener. Perhaps the Obama administration is better to start with a "sketchy" broadly-based plan that can be fine-tuned as it is implemented, rather than Hank Paulson's three-page, half-baked bailout plan that had to be abandoned in a matter of weeks.

❑ **Restore the "uptick" rule."** This arcane little piece of regulation used to say that you can't "short-sell" a stock unless it is rising. Short-selling is betting that a stock will fall. If the stock rises you have to pay up, if it falls, you make money without actually having bought the stock. The uptick rule was instituted by Joseph P. Kennedy, the first SEC Commissioner, in 1937 to prevent excessive short-selling during the 1937 market drop. That valuable backstop against market plunges was done away with by

Chapter 7: Where Do We Go from Here?

the SEC last year. The result? Once a stock begins falling, institutional investors pound it with short-selling and drive it into the ground, sometimes devaluing perfectly solid stocks for no apparent reason other than quick cash.

What were they thinking? Is every piece of speculation now automatically relegated to the lowest common denominator? Must we give the stock market over to the circling vultures of pessimism rather than those who seek to build new ideas and technologies? Just one more example of how an unregulated market feeds on greed and becomes a destroyer of value.

Throughout 2007 and 2008, top figures on Wall Street pleaded with the SEC to reinstate the 70-year-old rule. Some of the comments were: "we have never seen volatility like this," "decisive action cannot wait," "failure to reinstate the uptick rule is not acceptable." The SEC did nothing.

Many don't want the uptick rule restored. The reason? These guys have been making easy money for the last six months betting on failure by short-trading failing companies. (easy to pick: any company not being bailed out). One reason the market tanked on Timothy Geithner's recovery plan unveiling was that a recovery will make "short" trading more difficult, not necessarily, as was reported, that "the plans lacked specifics." With the recovery plan now in place, the emphasis for the next months and years will go back to stock picking (harder to do; that's why Wall Street was upset). Rising stocks will be those companies best positioned for surviving a weak market. Restoring the downtick rule would give these struggling companies a longer horizon to build success on than just "today's stock close."

❏ **Back on what track?** What track are we trying to get the economy back on? Republicans didn't like the stimulus plan because it didn't have enough short-term spending and tax cuts. That looks suspiciously similar to the track that got us here. For once in our entitled lives, perhaps we should be thinking more about producing than consuming. Economist and former Clinton Labor Secretary, Robert Reich talks about "the four horsemen of the apocalypse: widening inequality; dependence on foreign oil; crumbling infrastructure, and healthcare and education systems." Without fixing these, long-term prosperity will not really happen, and our role in the world will be a much diminished one. Allocating money for "structural" spending to address these problems is money well-spent. Yes, it will be very expensive, and, yes it will make the deficit much worse. But, even if we can't pay it back, at least now we will finally be borrowing money for things of lasting value instead of just instant gratification. It's a start.

Chapter 7: Where Do We Go from Here?

The Marketing Character

> *"Don't tell my mother I work in an advertising agency —
> she thinks I play piano in a whorehouse."* — Jacques Seguela

In 1955, Erich Fromm described the debut of the "marketing character," a one-dimensional, robotic, all-consuming character, who is well-fed, well-entertained, but passive, un-alive. and lacking in feeling.

Vancouver Sun writer, John Schumacher, describes Fromm and others of his generation, who envisioned the 21st century as a great age of enlightened thinking devoted to authenticity, social equality, and anti-materialism. In this vision we would revere nature, care about the welfare of coming generations, and reject dehumanizing bureaucratic and corporate authority. Something happened along the way.

Shumacher goes on to describe how the consumer culture has seduced us to disown our higher selves and enter the pointless dreamland of trinkets and desire. "Human potential has taken a backseat to economic potential and self-actualization has given way to self-absorption on a spectacular scale." Shallow "pop culture" has flourished as the masses were successfully duped into dedicating themselves to unceasing material overkill. In the dense fog of life in the fast lane, meaningful and meaningless are easily reversed. "Can a highly trivialized culture, marooned between fact and fiction, and dizzy with distraction and denial, elevate its values and priorities in order to respond effectively to the multiple planetary emergencies looming today"? Schumacher points to "culture change strategists" such as Jan Lundberg who are able to inspire leaps of consciousness independent of hapless "follow-the-leader" politics.

Lundberg warns that hyper-consumerism trivializes reality and numbs people even to the prospects of their own survival. He writes: "Unless we broaden and deepen our perception of both the universe and our fellow members of society, we all may perish in persisting to manipulate each other and our ecosystem with materialism and exploitation."

The article closes with Schumacher cautioning: "The cultural indoctrination race is not over. The losers are still winning and the odds for a revolution of consciousness are no more than even. But is there an alternative other than to drown in our own shallowness?"

Chapter 7: Where Do We Go from Here?

The Final Word

> *"If we go on the way we have, the fault is our greed [and] if we are not willing [to change], we will disappear from the face of the globe, to be replaced by the insect."*
> — Jacques Cousteau

Uncharacteristic of this book, I'm going to give the final words to a guru of finance. Perhaps I'm granting this dubious honor because this guru spent her formative years as a waitress. Celebrity investor Suze Orman was fielding calls on a recent NPR call-in show about the economy, when a twenty-something called, asking about the future. "Every generation has always improved their station in life," he said. "With things going as they are, will we ever have more than our parents?" Orman thought for a few seconds before she answered. "Yes," she said, "you will have something your parents never had. You will live within your means."

— About the Author —

Doug Friesen was born and raised on the prairies of Canada in a family of seven, where he spent his youth working for the family's community newspaper.

In his twenties and thirties, Friesen built energy-efficient homes. In the early 1980s, drawn by America's "tremendous opportunity," he moved to Boston. Soon after, he founded Duxborough Designs, a home design and construction business, and became a naturalized U.S. citizen.

Friesen lives on Boston's South Shore with his wife, Lois. where he is actively involved in his church and community life.

Printed in the United States
214842BV00001B/2/P